BUYING A SHOP

BUYING A SHOP

The Daily Telegraph Guide

Third edition

A ST J PRICE

Kogan
Page

First published in 1976 by A St J Price.
Second edition 1979; third edition 1986, both
published by Kogan Page Ltd, 120 Pentonville Road,
London N1 9JN.

British Library Cataloguing in Publication Data

Price, A. St. J.
    Buying a shop: a Daily Telegraph guide.—3rd ed.
    1. Stores, Retail—Great Britain—Purchasing
    I. Title
    333.33'8   HD1393.26.S8

    ISBN 1-85091-108-8

Printed and bound in Great Britain by
Dotesios (Printers) Limited
Bradford-on-Avon, Wiltshire

Contents

Introduction

Each year thousands of people buy a shop for the first time — and promptly wish they hadn't. They are landed with a bad decision and are often forced to resell at a substantial loss.

The results are heartbreak and a waste of resources. A substantial proportion of the businesses for sale at any time are on offer because the owners are disillusioned. The several reasons include:

- They have been 'sold a pup'.
- They do not like the trade, on close acquaintance with it.
- The business was a reasonable buy, but they lack the knowledge or experience to run it successfully.
- They paid too high a price, or borrowed too heavily, and the proposition is not viable financially.

All these mistakes can be avoided

With the help of this book, you can avoid the major mistakes and most of the minor ones. Of course you will make a few — that is how one learns — but they will be less serious and, being forewarned, you will minimise the resulting problems. You will increase your chances of success in business because you will be leaving far less to luck than the average buyer. You will be asking yourself, and other people, those questions the people who failed never thought to ask. The military adage that reconnaissance is seldom wasted applies equally to business. Time spent asking the right questions always pays off.

This book will not, of course, make the decisions for you. Every project reaches a stage when there has been enough thought and it is time for action. There is no substitute for experience. What the book will do is to stop you rushing in without thinking things through. It will vastly improve your ability to spot what is wrong with a proposition.

Franchised shops are not dealt with specifically in this book, but the same problems arise plus the necessity for a contract with the franchisor, which should be handled through a solicitor.

If you can answer 'yes' to every question that is asked in this book, you are not only a paragon, you have probably spent too long already thinking rather than acting. One can never cover every aspect of a deal, nor be 100 per cent certain. So do not worry if you have to leave some points uncovered. But try to meet as many as you can — the more you answer 'yes', the more risks eliminated.

Above all, do please take outside skilled advice. It is always worth paying the fees of a good adviser. If he stops you making a bad deal, it is a cheap way of avoiding all the worry of a failure. If he advises in favour, his advice need make only a marginal improvement to the terms, or to your plan of action, for the benefits to cover the cost.

A St J Price, FCA
Cirencester
August 1985

Chapter 1

Have You and Your Family Thought about Yourselves?

The telephone rang. 'Can I have details of the sweet shop you are advertising?' said the young lady at the other end. 'It is still available, is it? We haven't missed it, have we?'

'No,' I said, and took down her address. 'Have you had a business before?' I asked.

'No,' she replied, 'but this one sounds just right. I do hope we're in time to get it.'

'Steady on,' I said, 'what's the hurry?'

'Oh, but you see,' came the excited reply, 'it's me and my mum. We've just inherited £4000 and we're dying to have our own business. Actually we haven't got the money yet, but the shop you're advertising sounds the very thing we want and we're so anxious not to miss it!'

By now I knew that the business on our books was not the right one for them.

'Relax,' I said, 'this isn't the only business around. If you miss it, there will always be others. Certainly, I'll send you the particulars and you can go and see it, but you'd be wise to take it more slowly, learn a bit about shopkeeping and see a few businesses before you choose. If you'd like to bring your mother in for a talk, we can discuss the subject generally and help you both sort your ideas out before you rush into bidding for a particular business.'

She sounded a charming lass. I never saw her, or her mum, so I can only hope that they took some note of my advice because they were the typical 'innocents', ripe to be taken to the cleaners by anyone with a poor quality business to unload. They knew so little and were in such a breathless hurry that they did not stand a chance when up against an experienced business person.

Few agents would have taken the trouble to calm them down and encourage sensible thinking. It is the job of the agent to sell businesses on behalf of his client and theoretically I was acting against the interests of mine in putting off a possible purchaser. In the harsh reality of business life, I have found that such an approach does not really pay the agent; the more 'innocent' people are, the more unwilling they are to do their homework or pay for a little advice; worse still, when one tries to offer such advice, instead of just selling them the first business for which one can persuade them to part with their cash, they suspect one's intentions.

It was to try to help first-time buyers that I wrote this book. So many of those who contact me have not progressed much further than a feeling that it would be 'nice to have a little shop'. When asked about the trade, type of shop, location, price and so on, they have only the vaguest idea; sometimes they even resent being asked any questions. Frankly, at that stage, they are a menace, both to themselves, their families and to society in general. They have little chance of finding the right sort of business at a price they can afford and of borrowing the necessary money, let alone making a success of the business once they own it.

You are different

Of course, you are different because you have had the sense to start reading this book. But you are not *that* different. Many of those who make a mess of buying a shop are intelligent people who just do not spot what later — when it is too late — becomes blindingly obvious to them. So let us begin at the beginning.

When you buy a business, you take on a new career and commit yourself to a 24-hour responsibility, very likely with property attached. Such a decision cannot be undone easily and it is therefore important to get it right. So what are the key questions you and your family should ask yourselves before you decide on the kind of business which you want?

Your skills, experience and knowledge

When considering the kind of business you want, it is common sense to look first at the skills, experience and knowledge which you and your family already have, and at any hobbies or part-time activities in which you or they take part. It is important that you should enjoy what you do, but experience and knowledge have to be paid for in one way or another. If you can use what you already have, this will save you both time and money. On the other hand, if you go into a trade merely as a way of earning a living, rather than because you enjoy it and like it as a job, you may find that the responsibility weighs heavily on you.

Equally, a business, which looks like an easy way of earning good money, is most unlikely to turn out that way. It only looks easy because you do not know enough about it.

Thus it is as important to understand the disadvantages of the trade as it is to know the advantages and to assess whether the good points outweigh the bad. For instance, a newsagent with a delivery round, or a baker who produces his own bread, has to be an early riser. Much of their work has to be done before the rest of the world gets up. Some people find it easy to get up early in the morning; others are night birds for whom the early hours would be a serious disadvantage.

Your health

Certain trades demand considerable physical exertion. Those cans of beans do not get on to the grocery store shelves by themselves; the weekly delivery from the wholesaler does not necessarily arrive when it is most convenient, and if you use a cash and carry wholesaler, off-loading is also your responsibility.

Your ambitions

Empire builders usually have to go where the customers are. Generally, this means the big cities and the main trading areas, or perhaps it means a run-down property in a neglected area where the conditions are poor but there is the opportunity to build up the business.

The country store attracts many who wish to opt out of the rat race, or to work for themselves in the few years before, or immediately after, retirement. It may well offer a reasonable income in pleasant surroundings but prospects are likely to be limited. If the business has been neglected, you may be able to build it up considerably but even so, the potential will be restricted by the limited number of potential customers living close by. Once people get into their cars to shop, they do not normally use the village store, other than for minor purchases forgotten during the main shopping expeditions. Your ambitions may conflict with your desire for attractive surroundings.

What about yourself?

No one should buy their own business until they are quite sure that this is really what they want to do. We all have our dreams

11

and fantasies about life. They are a normal and healthy aspect of our personalities, but it is important to distinguish between that 'the grass is greener on the other side of the fence' feeling and a deeply held desire to do one's own thing. Because, when the going gets tough and the first flush of enthusiasm wears off, guts and determination may keep you going but ultimate success is not likely or will be a hollow achievement if you are unhappy working for yourself.

If you are not sure about this, try working for someone else in a small business first so that you can see what it is really like. In fact, this is a good idea for anyone before they go into a business for the first time, as is explained later.

Do not let me put you off!

I hope I am not making the running of a small business sound too frightening. Do not let me put you off, if you really want to have a go. In stressing the hard work and so on I am merely 'throwing a bucket of cold water at you' in your own interests.

The biggest single difference between working for someone else and owning your own business is summed up in that advertisement of the Industrial and Commercial Finance Corporation a few years ago. The entire newspaper page was blank except for these words:

'I resign'

'You can't, you're the boss'

How true! When you are the boss, nothing happens unless you make it happen. No longer do you have other people on whom you can rely for much of your daily routine. Executives in big companies are used to having their secretaries organise many details, the accounts department deal with much of the administration and other departments advise them on various aspects, such as advertising, printing, security, and so on. In a small business, you either buy such help in from outside or you do it yourself, which in effect means you do it yourself, since you cannot usually afford to buy it.

The list of questions at the end of this chapter covers various points, such as whether you like responsibility, organising your own working day, working by yourself and selling — the latter is particularly important. No one, but no one, helps the small businessman to sell. You will have to begin by selling yourself before you can sell your goods. Not many people are naturally good at selling themselves; but this is a skill which is central to the success of most businesses.

Do not underestimate the sacrifices which your family, in particular your spouse, may have to make if your business is to succeed. If he or she does not understand this in advance, the long hours and the physical toll on you will be an unpleasant surprise and will do your relations no good.

Working for yourself can be rewarding and profitable but it's always tougher than it looks.

Knowledge of your trade

Before you take the plunge, it is as well to appreciate what skills and knowledge your chosen trade requires. Every business has its own quirks, many of which can only be learnt by experience. For instance, it is theoretically possible for a newcomer to take over a greengrocer's shop with no previous experience; the wholesaler will deliver, there is little stock since the merchandise is sold fresh and cash turns over quickly. It looks like a good proposition until you realise that the best greengrocers do not buy from the wholesaler; they go to the market themselves (those dawn risings again!) and they select the produce with great care. As a result, they have the best of what is on offer and they then make the most of it by displaying it well. There is both skill and hard work involved in producing those shelves full of succulent-looking goodies which distinguish the outstanding greengrocer from the average. And it is the outstanding shop that makes good money. Most of the rest make a bare living, and no more.

Previous experience

My earlier remarks on the way most people approach buying their first shop are exemplified by their attitude to working for someone else first. I always suggest to those who come to me for advice that they should find a friendly shopkeeper in their area, who will employ them, perhaps at weekends or for an hour or two in the evenings, so that they can get some experience. They always agree to the idea in theory, but they do not put it into practice.

Buying your first shop is not normally a snap decision which has to be taken at once; when it is, it is probably a bad decision anyway. It is usually possible to spend some time planning

13

beforehand; indeed, it normally takes at least three months to find the right business, negotiate its purchase and complete the deal. Time spent working, in the interim period, for someone else in the same trade would give you invaluable experience. For one thing, you can see how someone else tackles the problem. There is never just one right way to do things in shopkeeping and it is very useful to see how different people approach ordering goods, stocking and displaying them, and all the many aspects of shopkeeping.

As a beginner, you are going to make some silly mistakes which experience will prevent you from repeating. This is unavoidable; it is merely a question of how you pay for them. In working for someone else, you may well earn little money and have to work hard, but this is a cheaper way of paying for knowledge than using your own money buying the wrong stock, acquiring unsuitable equipment or incurring unnecessary expense.

Here's a minor example of this. When they bought their first shop, Pat and Dave immediately installed a frozen food display cabinet. As they were so busy taking over and learning the business, they paid little attention to where the electrician put the switch for it but, even if they had, they would not have realised the mistake. It was put about three feet up on a wall because that happened to be a convenient spot. A week later, a big delivery of groceries came in and was stacked against this wall. A few hours later, the couple realised that the contents of the frozen food cabinet were no longer frozen because a carton of groceries, when stacked against the wall, had knocked the switch off. This blunder cost them over £500 in unsaleable frozen food. A more experienced person would probably have realised the danger.

Of course, a limited amount of experience working for someone else cannot teach you everything but it is surprising how many tips there are to be picked up from people in the trade. So, gain experience in other people's shops or businesses before launching your own. Ideally you should leave your existing job up to a year beforehand and perhaps work in several shops to gain experience. However, I know that most of you will be too impatient to accept this advice and even a few weeks learning from someone else is better than none at all.

Incidentally, do not count the one or two weeks' induction into your own business which the vendor may offer you as part of your deal with him. This can be valuable, but you cannot expect to learn very much from the vendor. The main point is to introduce you to the customers and to help you find your way around the stock and so on. There will be so many new things to learn about your own shop that you will not have time to talk much about the trade in general and, anyway, it is not up to the vendor to start teaching it to you at that stage. What you do not know by then, you are unlikely to learn properly from him.

Background research

You will be amazed how much information is available on your chosen trade, if you only look for it. There is a mass of statistics, surveys, forecasts and so on available, and trade journals and the like. The latter can be very useful; for instance, they report the opening of new shop premises. Visits to new businesses which are accessible to you would teach you much about the latest ideas in layout, presentation etc.

Ask your local librarian or the Small Firms Information Centre nearest to you. See Chapter 11 on sources of information.

A useful introduction to the business is given in *Running Your Own Shop* by Roger Cox (Kogan Page, 1985).

Opportunities for training

You may also be surprised at the amount of training which is open to you, either free or at a reasonable cost. I do not mean technical skills, which I assume you have already learnt from a previous job, but useful courses run by technical colleges, evening classes, or correspondence courses or, sometimes, courses run by wholesalers, who provide them as part of their marketing effort.

Basic financial knowledge

Every small businessman should be able to read a profit and loss account and a balance sheet and should understand the basic financial facts relevant to his particular trade. Many of them not only cannot read their own accounts, but also have only the haziest idea which are the key figures affecting their profits.

Various questions on finance are set out below. You can find the typical sales, profit margins and the like for your trade by researching at the local library, talking to your accountant and so on. Consult also *Understand Your Accounts* by A St J Price

(Kogan Page, 1986).

The point of understanding something about the money side is, of course, that you will fail in your business if you do not get this aspect right. You may have many reasons, other than money, for going into your own business, but all of them become irrelevant if you cannot pay the bills; and you are not going to be able to pay the bills unless you make enough profit and see that that profit results in cash in the bank. You will multiply your chances of achieving the necessary profit if you understand the basics of finance.

The point of the various detailed questions about the average sales and profit margins of a typical shop in your trade is that, unless you understand what the normal figures are, you will find it difficult to assess those quoted to you for any shop which you are thinking of buying. High profits may come from high sales and low margins or, conversely, large profit margins on lower sales. The net profit available to you will not be the same as that for the existing owner, unless your borrowing costs on bank loans, hire purchase agreements and so on happen to be the same. He may also have, in the accounts, motor expenses and other items, which are different from the ones you will incur, and it is important to be able to spot this.

Buying the shop is not the only capital outlay. You cannot trade without stock and you may have to put a considerable sum, over and above the purchase price, into building up stocks, if these have been run down prior to sale by the vendor, or if you expand the business. You will be in trouble if you fail to work this out in advance and, in consequence, do not organise the necessary finance.

There *is* a difference between gross profit and net profit, and one pound in the till is *not* a pound available for spending. Yet there are those who do not understand that, if a shop is trading on an average profit margin of 20 per cent, £80 out of every £100 of sales has to go straight to pay the suppliers of the goods needed to replace the items which have been sold. Moreover, there are many other expenses, such as rent, rates, electricity, telephone, insurance, professional fees and the wages of any staff, which must be deducted from the remaining £20 before there is anything left for the owner.

The story which the annual accounts of the business have to tell you is an important one. Few small businessmen understand it properly which is one reason so many either fail or merely scrape a living.

Questions on Chapter 1

1. What skills, experience and knowledge
   (a) do you have?
   (b) does your family have?

2. What hobbies or spare-time activities do you have?

3. In deciding on the type of business, have you considered how you could exploit your existing knowledge?

4. What do you enjoy doing?

5. Are you really interested in your chosen trade or will it be merely a bread ticket?

6. Do you understand its disadvantages as well as its advantages?

7. Have you and your family listed the pros and cons and decided that the pros outweigh the cons?

8. Are you physically strong enough to handle the stock, cope with the hours etc?

9. What are your ambitions
   (a) to build an empire with big profits but large responsibilities?
   (b) to obtain a reasonable income in pleasant surroundings but with limited prospects?
   (c) well, you tell me!

10. How important to you are the conditions and surroundings in which you live?

11. Are you sure you really want your own business above all else? Are you sure this is not a passing fancy, or something to try out, or a means of escape from reality, which will lose its attraction as soon as the initial fun wears thin?

12. Do you like the responsibility of taking decisions?

13. Do you like organising your own working day?

14. Do you think the risk of financial loss is worth the chance of running your own affairs. Can you cope with the financial worries?

15. Do you like working alone?

16. Do you enjoy selling yourself?

17. Can you cope with long hours of work and, in the early years, few holidays?

18. Do you really want to be independent enough not to miss the security of a job?

19. Do your family understand the sacrifices which they will have to make and will they back you 100 per cent? Do they realise that, in the early years and/or at certain times, they may have to take second place to the business if it is to succeed?

20. What skills or knowledge does your chosen trade require?

21. Must you acquire them before you start or can you learn them by experience? Have you talked to people in the trade about this?

22. Can you obtain experience
    (a) of small shopkeeping in general
    (b) of your trade in particular
        by working for someone else before you start on your own?

23. Have you asked the local librarian what books, reports, statistics and other information he can produce about your chosen trade?

24. Are training facilities available from
    (a) other firms?
    (b) technical colleges?
    (c) evening classes?
    (d) postal courses?

25. Do you understand the basic financial facts of your trade, ie
    (a) average sales of a typical shop?
    (b) profit margins available?
    (c) costs of running a typical shop?
    (d) average net profit of a typical shop?
    (e) average stock turn and value of cash tied up with stock?

26. Do you understand the difference between gross profit and net profit?

Chapter 2

Have You Found the Right Professional Advice?

Instinctively, most of us hate paying for professional services. Partly this is because many professions do not advertise themselves and, as a result, their marketing is appalling and they have not properly explained the benefits of using their professional services. Accountants are particularly guilty of this. As a result many people do not understand what an accountant can do for them.

I must, therefore, ask you to take it on trust that it is worth finding good professionals and worth paying for their services. When I was financial director of a small industrial company, my responsibilities included the insurance of our factory and various other risks. I spent a great deal of time understanding what these risks were and discussing with the insurance company how best to deal with them. Not knowing much about insurance, I spent a lot of time learning and, since I dealt with only one insurance company, I had nothing with which to compare their advice. Our parent company then instructed us to use a firm of insurance brokers. I protested that this was unnecessary but was overruled. Once we started working together, I found the relationship most useful. They obtained better cover for us at similar cost, even after allowing for their commissions. These had to be added to the premiums, as we were no longer dealing direct with the insurance company. The brokers saved me a great deal of time and the company was better insured for the same money.

The moral is that good professional advisers are worth hunting for. You cannot take the value of their services for granted; you may have to show them that you understand good service and expect to get it but in the long run it is usually cheaper to use them rather than do the work yourself. You have only so much time available and, unless you happen to be knowledgeable about something like insurance or accounting, valuable time which would be better spent running other aspects of your business will be tied up in learning.

Some professions do not allow advertising and it is thus very difficult to assess the relative merits of different firms. However, once you have found someone you can trust, say a bank manager, you can ask for his advice on choosing firms. Theoretically, he will not recommend one firm against another but in practice he will always give you some hints.

Professional firms and banks are almost entirely a matter of people. There is very little difference on paper in the services which they offer; it is the people they employ who do a good or an indifferent job. The earlier you start to find the right professional help the better. Even though you may be a year or more off starting in business, you may obtain valuable advice on your plans, which will help you bring them to fruition more effectively. In any case, it is before you start that you have time to search out the right people.

Do not be afraid to see more than one firm in a particular profession and to ask for an estimate of their fees in advance. They may be reluctant to give this, claiming that it is a matter of how much time they have to spend on your affairs. This is true but your accountant, for instance, should be able to make a sensible guess if you give him a proper estimate of your basic figures and as much information as possible.

You can tell a certain amount from the look of the professional offices. If these convey a dusty image, the attitude of the partners is probably somewhat similar. I believe that it is worth looking for a small firm which is young and hungry when you are yourself small. They are more likely to understand your ideas and will work harder for you.

That, however, is not the same as going to a cut-price firm. In accountancy in particular, there are many firms or individuals who claim to produce accounts but who have no professional qualification to do so. Unless such a firm has an outstanding reputation locally, it is better avoided in favour of one whose partners are either chartered accountants (FCA or ACA) or certified accountants (FCCA or ACCA). People who style themselves simply accountants either have a junior diploma or none at all. Part of the price you pay to the qualified accountant represents the considerable cost to him of keeping up to date. His professional body expects him to devote a substantial part of his time to attending courses on, or reading about, the latest changes in tax law and the like. His qualification is your guarantee that, not only did he once pass examinations, but that he has maintained his standards since.

Qualifications by examination for insurance brokers are a

relatively new development and they often possess none. I advise avoiding those who do not have a proper office and preferably your broker should be a member of the British Insurance Brokers Association.

It is difficult to bring an element of competition into your choice of, say, your bank manager. He is included among the professionals because it is above all a service which he offers you — or it should be. Do not hesitate to take your proposition around more than one bank. Do not necessarily be overcome with gratitude because the first manager you see is prepared to offer you a loan. Banks may not like the idea of you touting your proposition around but they can scarcely complain since they advertise the merits of their respective services. Make sure you understand the basis of the charges which you will have to pay and, again, try to judge your man as well as your bank.

Questions on Chapter 2

1. Have you found a
   (a) bank manager?
   (b) accountant who should be qualified either as Chartered (FCA or ACA) or Certified (FCCA or ACCA)?
   (c) solicitor? No unqualified person can call himself a solicitor.
   (d) insurance broker? He should work from a proper office, not his home, and be a member of the British Insurance Brokers Association.

2. Are these advisers alert and interested in your business?

3. Do they seem to understand your problems and to offer sensible advice?

4. Do you get prompt attention to your requests for help?

5. Are their offices bright modern places or dusty cobwebbed corners?

Chapter 3
Do You Understand Your Finances?

People can be very amateurish in their approach to their business finances. When they ask for details of the businesses for sale, many do not know how much cash they can raise. It is as if they were talking about some children's game, not the hard world of business. You, I hope, will be more professional in your approach.

Sort out as many of the answers on finance as you can *before* you make an offer for a particular business. For one thing the range of choice available to you depends on them. You can only get an actual loan or mortgage once you have a specific property in mind, but you can clarify in advance who will lend to you in principle and on what basis.

Once you start negotiating for a particular business, you are likely to incur costs of various kinds for surveys, solicitor's fees etc, not to mention all the upset of preparation for a move, change of job etc. If you fix the money in advance as far as you can, you will avoid wasting time and cash on deals you cannot possibly finance. Many sales fall through for lack of cash and often the problem would have been obvious at the start, had the purchaser done his homework.

Many of the questions below are self-explanatory. In asking you how much you need for the purchase price of the business, I am raising a hypothetical question until you find the actual business; nevertheless, study of the particulars of typical businesses, which might suit you, would give you a fair idea of the likely price range.

Stocks

Many particulars quote a price 'plus SAV'. This means 'stock at valuation'. It is wise to allow a safety margin over and above the estimated figure for this, because you will only know the actual total on the day of takeover, when it is a little late to find that you are short of the necessary money.

Moreover, the quantity of stock which you take over will

probably have been reduced by the vendor, whether or not by agreement with you. It makes sense for him to let stocks run down, in order that you can buy in fresh stock and so reduce the problem of counting on the date of takeover.

As soon as you are in charge, you will have to buy in stocks to raise the level to normal. These purchases will have to be paid for on trade terms, ie at 30 days or the end of the following month, or on the spot if you use a cash and carry warehouse.

New equipment

You may also have to find extra cash for new equipment, vehicles etc since the vendor will naturally not have spent any unnecessary money in the last year or so, and the property is likely to need internal and/or external redecoration. If it is leasehold, the landlord may well be able to insist on this under the terms of the lease.

Removal expenses and your living expenses for the first few weeks are items which must not be forgotten. You must allow a little time to build up sales before you start drawing money out of the business.

Sources of finance

Most of the sources listed in the questions on pages 29-31 are obvious. Your bank is the first place to go — it will also be your cheapest source.

Nowadays it is less common for local businessmen to lend money to others because few of them have spare capital, but the possibility is well worth investigating. If you know anyone who is successful enough in business to have some spare cash, he could prove an understanding 'sugar daddy' since he will have been through the same process himself.

Borrowing from a finance house is always very expensive. A finance house is *not* a bank; it is a 'secondary' lender using money, which it has itself borrowed either in the 'money market' of the City of London or from businesses and individuals who have substantial sums of spare cash to deposit with it. In either case, it will be paying high rates for its money and that money will be correspondingly more expensive to you, more expensive than if you obtain it from a bank. Finance houses vary considerably in their substance and standing, many of them being subsidiaries of major banks. Always have your solicitor check the loan agreement before you sign it.

Sometimes local suppliers of goods will lend money. In certain areas, the wholesalers of newspapers will help finance newsagents in order to obtain their business; the same is true of breweries who will lend to clubs, free houses, restaurants and the like, provided that they obtain sole rights to supply the beer.

Building societies are the least likely source of finance. It is unusual for a society to lend against business property, though where this is freehold and includes living accommodation of high quality, it is occasionally done.

Security

Unfortunately potential lenders are not likely to pay much attention to the business which you are buying as a form of security. If it includes freehold property they will lend against this but, if you fail, the goodwill and assets of the business are likely to be worth very little. Security is supposed to be a protection against your failure to keep up the repayments and lenders therefore look for value which they can realise, no matter what happens to the business.

A long lease can sometimes be used for security but this depends upon the terms; it would normally need to be for at least, say, 21 years in order to offer something of substance to sell to another businessman.

The minimum cash you need to live on

When working out your finances, you will have to estimate how much you and your family need to live on. Food, clothes and other essentials, plus existing private hire purchase or mortgage payments, can add up to a substantial sum in relation to the taxable profits of the business you are buying.

If you live away from the business, you will have running costs for your home such as rent, electricity and telephone, as well as travelling expenses to the shop. All this is additional to the actual costs of running the business itself, which are allowed for in calculating the business profits.

When living accommodation is attached to the shop, the telephone will usually be charged to the business and you should enquire whether the accounts of the vendor show the full cost of the telephone, the rates, electricity and so on. If a part has been included in his drawings for the business, you will have to allow for it in your calculations because the profit shown in the accounts is before drawings. The latter are a distribution of profit to the owner, not a charge in the accounts. If part of the rates etc relate to the private accommodation, this is sometimes apportioned between business and private in the accounts rather than adjusted later.

If you live away from the shop, you can probably have a proportion of your telephone calls and the cost of the rental allowed against your profit. Your travel costs in getting to the business, however, are not allowable for tax under any circumstances, but remember to budget for them.

The cash available from the business

The cash available is the net profit, arrived at after charging up the expenses of the business *plus* depreciation. Though this is charged in the profit and loss account, it is not a cash expense. From the profit plus depreciation, you must deduct the cost of any equipment or other assets or any extra stock which you will need to buy. Allow for personal taxation on the profit as another deduction. The balance is the *cash*, as compared with the *profit* which will be available to you.

We will assume you are not trading as a limited company but, if this is the case, the profits of the company will be taxed separately from your own income; you may well draw all the company's profits as salary in which case they are taxed under PAYE.

Your accountant will explain your tax position in more detail and when you will have to make the payments. The timing is an important factor because initially there is a long delay before any tax is due.

What is left to repay the loans?

The money available to repay the loans is the cash less your living expenses. Thus if the business is producing £10,000 cash per annum less £2000 tax and you have living expenses of £7000, there is only £1000 available to pay the interest and to make repayments of capital for any loans.

In your first year, you will have no income tax to pay because business profits are assessed for tax in arrears on the profits of the previous year. In subsequent years, a payment is due each time.

The interest on the money you borrow for your business is allowable against the profits before tax is charged; so is interest on a mortgage or loan to buy a private house (provided the sum borrowed is under £30,000). The capital repayments, however, are not allowable for tax purposes on either business or private loans.

If you are a director of your own company, private mortgage interest is allowed in assessing your personal tax on the salary you draw, not against company profits.

Matching borrowing to assets

Long-term assets, such as property, should be financed by long-term loans. Equipment etc which wears out may be bought on hire purchase, leased, or rented. Bank overdrafts should be used for short-term payments, such as stocks and debtors. An overdraft is repayable overnight, should the bank demand it. The principle is to borrow long term the money you need for long-term items. This rule is often broken and sometimes businessmen get away with doing so. Sometimes, however, it is a mistake which bankrupts them. The following paragraphs discuss each kind of finance in more detail.

The difference between hire purchase, leasing and renting

Under a *hire purchase* agreement, you buy an item in instalments made up partly of interest, partly of the purchase price.

Under a *leasing* agreement, you pay for the cost of the asset, plus interest, in much the same way as on your hire purchase agreement, but you never actually own the item. The agreement may provide for you to be credited with the market value of it at the end of the lease; usually, you have the right to continue leasing it for a nominal sum. Leases normally last three to five years.

Renting is less common and simply means that you have the use of the asset under an agreement which may well last for no more than a year or so. Small items of business equipment, however, are not usually worth very much second-hand, and rental agreements tend to be for three or five years and to be used for goods such as telephone systems, telephone answering machines etc. Under the rental agreement, you have no rights over the equipment of any kind once the agreement is terminated. On the other hand, you usually have the right to end the rental agreement yourself, subject to whatever penalties it may contain.

Whatever the kind of agreement, always check the terms under which you can terminate it. Often these are penal so you should never commit yourself for, say, three years, unless you are sure that the goods will be usable for at least that time. For simple items of shop equipment that sounds a point hardly worth making — of course they will. But some things, such as computers, rapidly become obsolete. Even a shop's decor in, say, a boutique, can become outdated and unfashionable all too quickly.

Remember too that you will remain liable for payments under agreements uncompleted, if your business fails or you have to close it because of some disaster. It is sensible to be cautious about your borrowing to start with — do not go in too heavily until you have some trading experience and are sure of what you need and of your ability to earn the cash to pay for it.

Bank overdrafts and bank loans

A bank overdraft is instantly repayable. A bank loan is a fixed sum made for a fixed period, usually with regular repayments provided for, which include interest. The merit of a bank loan is that once made it cannot be recalled by the bank, provided you keep up the agreed payments. On the other hand, it has a higher interest rate because the bank has committed itself for a fixed period, often as long as seven years. If you know that you will have to borrow money from the bank for several years, a bank loan is much safer than an overdraft, because you cannot be caught out by a sudden credit squeeze.

An overdraft *limit* is the maximum you may borrow. Naturally the bank does not expect this sum to be borrowed all the time and it likes to see the actual level fluctuating and, better still, the account sometimes in credit as money comes in and out of your business. Incidentally the bank used by the vendor of your business may be more willing to lend than others, because it already knows the figures at first hand.

Borrowing from family and friends

There is a saying that if you borrow from a business contact, you should write out the terms agreed between you; if you persuade an acquaintance to lend you money, have your solicitor draw up the agreement; even if it is your brother who produces the money, make sure you sign it.

Money is a great breaker of social and family relationships. Do not be casual about your financial arrangements with your friends and relatives. Aunt Nelly may not understand that, having loaned money to you for your business one year, she cannot simply ask for it back in order to lend it to another nephew as the whim takes her. This is an extreme example of the sort of problem which arises, but it is essential that everyone understands from the start how long the money is to be borrowed for and on what basis it is to be repaid.

Rates of interest

A flat rate of interest sounds much lower than it really is. What it means is that, if you borrow £100 at 10 per cent flat rate with repayments over ten years, the true rate of interest is about double, ie 20 per cent. This is because the 10 per cent (£10) is payable for all ten years, although the sum outstanding is being reduced. Thus you pay £20 per year, half interest and half capital so that, after five years, there is only £50 outstanding. Yet you are still paying £10 of interest at the flat rate, which is now 20 per cent on the sum still owing.

All lending agreements should state the true rate of interest which is calculated on the average sum outstanding during the loan, not on the original sum borrowed. It is the true rate which should be compared with a bank overdraft rate or a building society mortgage.

Questions on Chapter 3

1. How much money do you have
   (a) in cash?
   (b) in property, shares, insurance policies, jewellery etc which you can sell or borrow against?

2. How much money do you need for
   (a) the purchase price of the freehold or leasehold of the property, equipment, fixtures, fittings and goodwill of the business, plus legal fees?
   (b) stocks of goods for resale, which you will take over from the vendor?
   (c) additional stocks you may have to buy to fill the shelves (allowing for any trade credit obtainable from suppliers)? Many vendors will run down stocks so as to reduce the starting cash needed but stocks have to be increased to normal levels by you.
   (d) new equipment, new vehicles, urgent major repairs, etc?

(e) initial expenses, such as removal costs, and running expenses until the business is paying its way?

The figures you need for this answer will vary a bit from business to business but study of the particulars of different propositions should give you a good basis for preliminary estimates.

3. In making these forecasts, have you allowed a safety margin for contingencies and unforeseen items?

4. How much does this leave you to borrow?

5. Have you tried the following possible lenders and clarified the terms on which they would lend to you?
   (a) your bank?
   (b) family and friends?
   (c) local businessmen?
   (d) finance houses?
   (e) your life assurance company (against your policies)?
   (f) local suppliers of the goods you will sell?
   (g) building societies? Although they will sometimes mortgage living accommodation with a shop attached, in general they avoid this sort of property.

6. What security can you offer?
   (a) house or business property freehold (or possibly a lease over, say, 21 years)?
   (b) life assurance policies?
   (c) shares in public companies quoted on the Stock Exchange?
   (d) jewellery?

7. How much cash per week do you need to live on, ie for food, clothes and other essentials, and existing private hire purchase or mortgage payments?

8. What profit do you expect the business to earn before income tax, but after paying all business expenses?

9. How much cash will be left to repay your loans, ie short-term assets such as stock on overdraft; long-term ones such as property against fixed loans?

10. Have you matched your borrowing to your assets?

11. Do you understand the difference between a bank overdraft and a bank loan?

12. Have you agreed an overdraft *limit* which leaves a safety margin above the actual amount you need?

13. If borrowing, *especially* from family and friends, have you signed a formal agreement?

14. Do you understand the difference between a flat rate of interest on a sum you borrow and the true rate?

15. Do your borrowings leave you a safety margin? Or are you borrowing up to the hilt, so that any temporary problem which arises will cause a crisis which will inhibit your business (if it does not make it go bust)?

16. If you have a house to sell, have you asked your bank manager whether he will provide bridging finance, if necessary from the date you pay for the business until that on which you receive the proceeds of your sale?

Chapter 4
Who Will Own the Business?

Who owns the business can be very important as soon as anything goes wrong; and if everything goes right and there are good profits, the ownership will decide who is entitled to those profits, or at least to the proceeds of selling the business, should you dispose of it in due course.

If you operate on your own, you are known as a 'sole trader'. A partnership has two or more people running the business together; a limited company is a separate legal entity. It is owned by its shareholders and run by its directors. It must have two shareholders but need have only one director, plus a company secretary who has certain legal functions. A 'sole trader' can therefore form a limited company with, say, his wife as the second shareholder and acting as the company secretary.

Each way of trading has advantages and disadvantages.

The perils of partnerships

Many small business partnerships do not last very long because of the strain on personal relationships. The partners need not be socially compatible; indeed, it is often easier if they do not meet after hours and if the relationship is purely a business one. But they must be able to agree on matters of policy and they must be able to work together in harmony.

Partnerships often break up because one partner feels that the others are not pulling their weight, are doing poor quality work, are concealing some of the takings, are adopting policies of which he disapproves, etc. When there are only two of you in the business, there is little room for disagreements of this sort.

You must have the utmost trust in each other, since you are each responsible for all the debts of the partnership. If a partner disappears, you will have to pay up and your only recourse is to sue him, when you can find him. Many of the problems of partnerships can be avoided, first by taking some care to get to know the others in business before joining forces, and second by having your solicitor draw up a partnership agreement. The points which this should cover are listed in the questions on page 35. Many of them are easy enough to resolve beforehand, but any one can become a source of profound disagreement if left to chance.

There may be tax advantages in making your wife or husband a partner. Ask your accountant about this.

Limited companies

A good deal of rubbish is talked about the advantages of trading as a limited company. Broadly speaking, until your profits approach £20,000 per annum, there is little to choose between the relative tax advantages of being a sole trader or incorporating yourself. Your accountant can explain this in more detail.

A company is limited because in theory it offers limited liability to the shareholders. In practice, however, you are likely to have to give your personal guarantee to your bank, if it lends you money, and possibly to any finance company or similar lender with whom you deal. This means that your personal assets are at risk to the extent of that guarantee, just as if you were a sole trader; only against the ordinary creditors for goods, materials etc do you have any degree of protection.

Limited liability can be very useful in certain special cases. These are mainly where the business carries a very heavy contingent liability. For instance, if you manufacture a food product which could conceivably cause customers to become ill, you have a contingent liability, however remote, which is huge. You should be insured against this but it is the kind of risk which might make it worthwhile to be limited.

Prestige is another reason for having a company. Neither this, nor the contingent liability problem, really applies to the small shop but in some businesses it does sound better to trade as a company. Those who know can usually tell whether the business involves anybody other than you and your spouse by looking at the letter heading, which must show the names of the directors. Nevertheless, prestige is perhaps something to be taken into account.

Once you have good profits, company tax law does allow you to leave a certain amount of money in the business; the tax restrictions on building up capital are a little less than those on a small trader or a partnership. It may also be easier to even out the tax bill for a limited company, if profits rise and fall substantially from one year to the next.

34

The disadvantages of forming a company are the extra legal costs involved and the expense and nuisance of filing annual returns each year. There can also be severe tax disadvantages, especially where you have to lend substantial sums to the business in its first year of operation. You may be unable to take this money back out of the business without incurring a heavy tax bill.

Having a company does mean that you can give, or sell, part ownership to your family, a friend, or a business acquaintance; on the other hand, such minority shareholders have fewer rights than junior partners and it may be impossible for a minority shareholder, who has lent money to the business, to get it back.

A limited company has to file its accounts annually with the Registrar of Companies where they are available for public inspection. Often this loss of privacy is unimportant in practice but, if your business is unusual or specialised, it could perhaps mean that useful information is available to competitors.

Losses in the early years of the business as a sole trader or a partnership can be offset against any other income which you have. There are certain more restricted possibilities for doing this if a loss is incurred by a company but, as a general rule, shareholders cannot offset losses against other incomes. Your accountant can advise you more fully on these and other points.

Questions on Chapter 4

1. Who will own the business?
   (a) you as a sole trader with your spouse as an employee?
   (b) you and your spouse as partners?
   (c) you and others as partners?
   (d) a limited company which you own (possibly in conjunction with others)?

2. Have you asked your accountant and your solicitor for advice on the relative advantages and disadvantages for you of each option?

3. If considering trading as a limited company, are you sure that you have assessed the pros and cons correctly? Some of these are as follows:
   Pros
   (a) Protection (from your unsecured creditors only) against bankruptcy due to failure. This can be important where major contingent liabilities or legal problems could arise

out of your activities.
(b) Ease of allocating a part of the business to others via shareholdings.
(c) A certain amount of prestige.
(d) Once profits are high enough for some money to be left in the business, the tax restrictions on building up capital are a little less than for a sole trader or a partnership.
(e) It may be easier to even out the tax bill for a limited company, if profits rise and fall substantially from one year to the next.

Cons
(a) Extra legal costs on formation and continuing cost of maintaining registration as a company.
(b) Extra paper work in complying with company law.
(c) In certain situations there are severe tax disadvantages, while the compensating advantages only begin to apply once profits are higher than the sums the owners need to live on.
(d) Minority shareholders have fewer rights than junior partners and they can find it impossible to get their money out.
(e) A limited company must file accounts which are available for public inspection.

4. If you are buying the business from a limited company, have you asked your accountant for advice on whether to buy the company itself (ie its shares from its shareholders) or whether you should take merely the assets (ie property or lease, fixtures, fittings and goodwill) from the company?

5. If you will be in partnership, has your solicitor drawn up an agreement covering such points as:
   (a) who pays how much of the purchase price.
   (b) If any money is being loaned by a partner, what interest will be payable and when the loan will be repaid.
   (c) What guarantee or security against personal assets is to be given by each partner. In principle each partner is liable for the *entire* business debts of the partnership. He can be made bankrupt for his partners' shares as well as for his own.
   (d) Who works in the business and who takes the decisions.

(e) Who draws what salary each week or month. In due course the annual accounts will show the actual profit and the drawings are an advance payment.

(f) How the annual profits or losses are to be shared.

(g) How any capital profit or loss made on the sale of the business, or part of it, is to be shared.

Chapter 5
Do You Know Your Trade?

Some of the questions in this chapter may seem a bit esoteric or over-elaborate, but you do not have to know *all* the answers; the point of asking the questions is to emphasise the need for the modern businessman to understand something of the wider scene in which he trades. If you do your homework, you will foresee important trends long before they make their greatest impact.

New developments, such as supermarkets, which revolutionise a trade, do not just happen. It usually takes years for them to grow. Wide-awake businessmen can spot such trends in time to take advantage of them. So do not be too parochial in your approach. Study your trade and use the mass of information available. Ask your local library or Small Firms Information Centre for details (see the sources of information, pages 96-8).

Prospects in your trade

This is perhaps the most important of the lot. There are fads and fashions in business, just as in other aspects of life. Launderettes are one example. Too many were opened with the result that many have either closed or make no more than a bare living. It is important to understand whether your chosen trade is expanding, or is static, or is thoroughly over-exploited and therefore declining, if not overall at least in average sales per shop or perhaps locally.

Video rental shops are a current example of a new business growing rapidly and therefore attracting more new people. Video shops have appeared all over the country. Will the trade go on expanding? If it does will main retailers such as W H Smith or Boots take it over, squeezing out many of the small shops? Are there now enough outlets or is there really room for more? How important will the right site be once the trade settles down? Such questions should be considered by anyone thinking of joining the rush into video.

The public interest

New laws on health, safety, hygiene and pollution are demanding higher standards in many trades. For instance, few small butchers now have their own slaughterhouses because the regulations require expenditure which it is uneconomic to make. An awareness of impending legislation, which may affect your trade, could save you from buying a business which will be unable to meet the new requirements, at least without substantial expenditure. Such legislation may also offer new opportunities; some slaughterhouses must be doing considerably more business with small butchers now forced to come to them.

Trends in new products

The launderette business was created by the availability of washing machines but at prices which the average household could not afford. Pocket calculators came from new technology. Both created new opportunities or even new businesses. Those opportunities changed however, even disappeared, once prices came down and most people owned a machine.

Stick to your last

As a young man, I once owned a confectionery and tobacconist shop. It was on a short lease and I was concerned about the possibility of moving it. A fish and chip shop in another part of the town came on the market; at first I looked at it as a possible site to which to move the business but, on seeing the figures, I decided that it looked very profitable as it was. I therefore bought it, without knowing anything about frying fish. My manager from the other shop ran it for a while but later we found a young couple to take it on. At this stage I had made several of the mistakes which I have warned you about, including taking on a business about which I knew nothing. We put quite a lot of money into improving the premises and creating a new dining room. Not only did we try to do lunches and suppers, but afternoon teas as well. The result was a mess — we were neither a fish and chip shop, nor a tea shop.

The moral is to be very careful before you mix two trades which are not normally found together. Fish and ships do not really go with tea and sandwiches, which is why they are not normally sold on the same premises.

Talk to local officials

The local Planning Officer and the Environmental Health Officer could both be very helpful to you.

The Planning Officer can tell you of local policy on where new shops are permitted or encouraged, where the Council is unlikely to allow development and which areas will be affected by major new schemes.

Your local Environmental Health Officer can tell you about the trends in hygiene, safety etc which affect your trade and about his own attitudes towards applying them in his area. Before you buy your business, it might be worthwhile talking to him about whether he is satisfied that it meets the standards required or whether he will use a change of ownership to demand improvements. He has considerable powers and discretion on how he uses them and his advice could be invaluable.

You may also need to have licences. For instance, bottles of milk cannot be sold by just anyone. Most of this sort of thing is straightforward enough but you do need to know the rules.

Will you be lending money or advising on it? Anyone who either lends money to the public or advises them on how to obtain a loan or mortgage etc needs a licence under the Consumer Credit Act. This does not apply to ordinary trade credit of a month or two granted to customers, but it does have a very wide application. If in doubt, check.

Will you employ people?

The Employment Protection Act is a much maligned piece of legislation. However, its complications can make life difficult for the small businessman if he does not understand the rules.

Once you have employed somebody for a while, you cannot just sack him/her at your whim. You can declare him/her redundant, if you no longer need an employee to do the job, but you may then have to make a redundancy payment.

The Advisory, Conciliation and Arbitration Service (ACAS), which is a government agency, can give you a great deal of help and advice on employment matters. Its services are free.

Pay As You Earn is not difficult to operate once you know how it works. If you are not familiar with it, it would be wise to ask somebody to show you before you take over the business, so that you are prepared. You have to deduct tax under PAYE when you employ staff, according to the tax code number they supply and subject to minimum limits set by each Budget. All deductions (income tax and National Insurance contributions) must be in accordance with the tables supplied by the local tax offices.

Value Added Tax

This is a further piece of legislation which needs to be taken seriously. People either take VAT very seriously and are scared stiff of it or they think they know all about it. They are usually wrong in both cases and it is not at all safe to take for granted what the previous owners of the business have done.

Some accountants provide VAT services for their clients but, even then, I advise some study of the law. See *VAT Made Easy* by A St J Price (Kogan Page, 1979).

Questions on Chapter 5

1. How much business can an average small shop in your chosen trade expect to do each week? Is your trade growing, static or declining?
   (a) nationally?
   (b) locally?

2. If your trade is not expanding, how will you make *your* business grow where other people are failing to do so?

3. Are there opportunities or problems in your trade because of
   (a) changes in fashion or public taste?
   (b) higher standards required by new laws?
   (c) higher standards demanded by public opinion?
   (d) new products or changing technology opening up fresh opportunities?
   (e) too many outlets in the trade — too many people have jumped on the bandwagon of a new trend?
       Launderettes are an example.

4. Are the supplies of goods readily obtainable? Some goods are sold only through dealers or there may be shortages.

5. Is your prospective local competition
   (a) efficient or inefficient?
   (b) thin on the ground or too numerous for all to prosper?

6. If there seems to be a gap in the local facilities for you to exploit, is it because
   (a) no one else has yet had a go?
   (b) others have tried and failed?
   (c) the situation is not what it seems?

7. What sort of people will be your customers
   (a) local people living close by?
   (b) people from a wide area?
   (c) collectors/sportsmen/specialists?
   (d) house buyers etc?

8. What quality of goods and how big a choice will they want?

9. Could you be making the mistake of trying to mix two types or levels of trade?

10. Have you looked at the premises of a wide range of other businesses in your trade? Are you aware of the latest trends in display methods and equipment? Do you know what such equipment can do and what it costs?

11. Have you contacted the Planning Officer about likely developments in your area?

12. Have you talked to the local Environmental Health Officer about trends in hygiene, safety etc affecting your trade, and about his own attitudes?

13. Do you know what licences you may require in your trade?

14. Do you know the outlines of the following laws and the extent to which they will affect your trade?
    (a) Consumer Credit Act
    (b) Employment Protection Act
    (c) PAYE
    (d) VAT

Chapter 6
How to Choose the Actual
Business – the Points to Consider

This chapter deals with selecting the right business. Assessing the price and negotiating the actual deal are dealt with later. Here we are simply concerned with whether or not it is a suitable business for you.

The questions on pages 42-43 assume that you have decided what sort of trade you want to be in, and that you may be looking for empty premises rather than a business which is already trading. Some of the points, therefore, concern assessing the value of a particular site for your purpose, as opposed to that for which it is presently being used.

Suppose you have decided to start a shop selling model kits. You are unlikely to find a suitable existing one because there are not very many such businesses. You will therefore be looking for empty premises to buy or rent.

A specialist shop of this nature can often be in a secondary shopping street or a suburban location because people will visit it as it is the only one of its kind in the area. This is not to say, however, that any position will do. People who come from a distance should be able to find your shop easily, and a nearby car park may well be important.

The difference between a specialist shop and one selling necessities, such as food, is that customers will seek out the specialist shop, whereas they tend to buy from the provider of necessities only if it is convenient for them to do so. They will choose a location which they pass regularly or to which they have easy access from their home or job.

It is worth spending a good deal of time on choosing your site and in talking to people in business about the problems involved. Siting is one of the more difficult things to get right but it is a key point to which successful businessmen pay a great deal of attention.

Little things can make a big difference to the value of shops even on opposite sides of the street. For instance, in York, one of the main bridges over the river has far more pedestrian traffic on one side than on the other. The reason is that the busy side leads to the main shopping street, turning left at the T junction at the city centre end. Turning right takes one down a secondary road. Consequently, the shops on the left side of the bridge, which leads to the main shopping centre, have a pedestrian flow past their doors several times bigger than the one on the other side.

This is obvious to anyone who watches carefully for a short while, but similar local factors are not always so obvious. So walk about and get to know the area, not just the street the shop is in. Consider taking advice from a local estate agent; he will act on your behalf for a fee.

Development plans

The local planning office will tell you about development plans in the area. These can be very important, not only because they may indicate future new business from new housing developments, factory extensions etc, but also because they may show that you will have great difficulty in obtaining permission to extend your business premises, assuming that you have the land on which to do so. If the area has been designated as residential, planning permission will not be easily come by, unless your extension happens to fit in with the shopping facilities which the planners have decided are necessary.

Incidentally, you should not assume that planning permission has been obtained for any development the previous owner may have made. This includes a new shop front or a sign which he may have put up. If the upper part of the premises is let separately as offices, is this in order? *He* may have been getting away with it but you should not count on doing so yourself.

Talking of planning leads on to fire regulations, hygiene requirements etc. In an earlier chapter I mentioned the need to be aware of current and forthcoming changes and again, you should not just assume that the premises currently comply with the law.

Other local shopping

Even though you are not in the city centre, it is worth trying to find a site in a good parade of shops or in an area which contains first-class basic facilities such as a post office and food shops. Good local stores support each other; a first-class butcher next to a greengrocer who knows his job will provide automatic business for a grocer and general store because people will come knowing that they can get good produce conveniently from all three.

Sub post offices

Because of the security which the sub postmaster's salary offers, this kind of business is in great demand and is correspondingly expensive. You should realise, however, that the postmastership is not automatically transferred to the buyer but is subject to the approval of the local postmaster. This is not automatic and can be withheld, theoretically because you are judged unsuitable, but more probably because the Post Office decides not to renew the contract. It has a policy of reducing the number of sub post offices and, before committing yourself to buy the business, you should therefore check that a transfer of the post office side of the operation is available.

The requirements are few for the position of sub postmaster. The main point is you must be able to manage the cash and make it balance. There is a certain amount of bookkeeping involved, so you must check exactly what the duties involve before deciding that this is for you.

A word of advice

Do look at as many businesses, similar to one you intend to buy, as you can before taking a final decision. This will help you put things into perspective and you will become more discriminating than you were when you first saw a 'valuable freehold business offering a secure income'.

Questions on Chapter 6

1. What sort of site is right for your plans? City centre? Suburbs? Housing estate? Country village? Main arterial road? Busy street? Back street? Immigrant area? Etc.

2. Can you draw customers because of the nature of the goods or service you offer or must you be placed conveniently where they live, work or pass by?

3. Is car parking important?

4. Can customers find and get to your shop easily on foot, by public transport or by their own means?

5. Have you counted the people passing the shop in shop hours, noted the sort of people they are, who the shop attracts etc?

6. Does the number of passers-by vary greatly from time to time or day to day?

7. Is the flow of passers-by mostly on one side of the street or the other? If so, is it *your* side?

8. What trends are shown by the population census for the area?

9. What development plans are there for the area which may affect trade?

10. Is the shop close to a post office, a newsagent, a baker, a butcher, a greengrocer etc? Will people be drawn to shop there?

11. Are the neighbouring shops well run, thus creating a good reputation for the area?

12. Does the shop itself have a basic draw, such as sub post office or newspapers, to attract customers?

13. Are the local schools right for your children?

14. Has the present owner been there a long time? Has there been a rapid succession of owners? If so, why?

15. Why is the present owner selling
    (a) retirement, health etc?
    (b) because he has failed in the business?
    (c) failure because not enough trade is available to make a profit?
    (d) because he sees trouble ahead which will reduce trade?

16. Have you *discreetly* chatted to neighbouring shopkeepers about their views on prospects both for the area and for the shop?

17. Have you talked to the local suppliers of the goods you will be selling?

18. Are there any restrictions applying to the property which would prevent your altering it as you might wish? Examples are:

(a) preservation order on building of historical interest.
(b) restricted trades allowed — usually part of a lease
(c) rights of way of neighbours
(d) planning restrictions on development of the area.
(e) planning restrictions on trades allowed in the area preventing you from changing its use.

19. If planning permission is required for any development or any use of the premises, has it in fact been obtained? This includes permission for any exterior signs for which the landlord's agreement may also be needed under the terms of the lease.

20. Are there any local authority orders not yet complied with concerning such matters as fire regulations, hygiene etc?

21. If buying a sub post office, will you be able to satisfy the requirements of the main postmaster who must approve you?

22. When is the post office salary due for review (every three years)? Is your holiday relief paid for by the Post Office?

23. Is it possible that, on a change of ownership, the Post Office will decide not to continue that particular sub post office?

24. Have you seen enough similar businesses to be able to distinguish their good and bad points?

Chapter 7

Leases – Do You Know the Pitfalls?

This chapter will interest you only if you buy a business in rented premises.

Remember that a lease is a legal contract and once you are in the premises you are bound by it. If you treat your lease as a mere boring formality, it may cost you a great deal of money later when you find you cannot do what you want or have perhaps to do what you do not want. So insist on reading it and ask your solicitor to explain it if necessary.

Sometimes, a tenant does not have a lease because he is a friend of the owner. Either no lease agreement was ever signed, or it was not renewed. This can be very dangerous for a new-comer. Security of tenure depends on your having a lease. While a landlord cannot terminate a business tenancy entirely at will, even if there is no formal agreement, he can nevertheless do so much more easily than with residential property. Here are five conditions under which a landlord can refuse to renew a lease under the Landlord and Tenant Act and can require possession.

1. He wants to redevelop the premises.
2. He wants to use the premises himself (but only if he has owned them for at least five years).
3. You have not paid the rent.
4. You have defaulted on some other obligation under the lease.
5. Your lease is a sub-tenancy and, when it expires together with the lease for the part occupied by your immediate landlord, the superior landlord can obtain more rent for the premises as a whole than for the individual parts.

Nowadays many leases are for short periods of three or five years. Where the premises are modern and purpose-built, the landlord is usually a developer or investor, who is unlikely to require the premises for his own use or to want to rebuild them. But this is not the case with older property, and you need to pay particular attention to this. The planning officer may advise you that the premises are a listed building, but this will not necessarily mean that it cannot be gutted and refurbished inside.

Use of the premises

Many leases contain restrictive covenants on the goods which may be sold, or the trades for which the premises may be used. Sometimes these are incorporated into all the leases in a parade of shops in order to regulate the competition between them. Such clauses may or may not be a dead letter depending on the situation and how long ago they were executed. One often finds that the vendor has been ignoring them, but your arrival may be just the opportunity the other tenants have been waiting for to stop your shop selling something.

Transfer of your lease

Some leases prohibit you transferring them to anyone else. This means that you would simply have to give up the premises and the person who bought your business would have to negotiate a fresh lease with the landlord. This would be a serious disadvantage when selling and would probably reduce the price which you could obtain for your business.

Case history

Mrs P and Mrs K approached me to sell their boutique. Well-placed in a city centre it had looked an exciting proposition when they paid £17,000 for it, plus stock at valuation. But what they actually got for their money was a few well-worn fittings, such as show stands, dummies, carpets etc. Most of the rest was goodwill because their lease made no provision for its transfer and so was only of value to them while the shop was profitable. The lease itself could not be sold to anyone else.

When they found the boutique business was more difficult than they thought and that sales were falling off from the figures claimed by the previous owner, they were in deep trouble. They had borrowed most of the purchase price and the repayments and interest left them nothing.

The landlord was thoroughly awkward and saw no reason to allow a transfer. He wanted to repossess the premises and relet them himself for a higher rent. I tried to make him offer a new lease to the prospective purchasers I found, so that we could at least salvage something. But he quibbled about their references and about the terms of the new lease, so they became disheartened and went off to negotiate less problematic deals elsewhere.

The result was that the business became unsaleable and the partners eventually had to vacate the premises. They had most of the original debt still around their necks. Much of the substantial quantity of stock left on their hands was now difficult to dispose of; it was 'fashion' garments now out of season and by next year it would no longer be fashionable.

What a disaster! They had originally paid far too big a price for a high risk business in which they were amateurs, but the problem was made worse by the lease.

What could have saved them was a clause, common to many leases, saying that they could transfer it to anyone subject to the consent of the landlord, such consent not to be unreasonably withheld. This wording means that in practice under such a lease, you can insist on the right to transfer provided that your transferee can produce satisfactory references.

Dilapidations

This is jargon meaning the premises may have deteriorated during the tenure of the vendor. The lease will provide for either the landlord or the tenant to repair and redecorate either the exterior or the interior of the premises or both, very likely at stated intervals. You should check your obligations on this point and see whether the vendor has fulfilled his.

Often a landlord will not worry about this until a change of tenancy. The result can be a hefty bill for dilapidations, ie the repairs and redecorations necessary to bring the premises up to the standard they were in when originally let.

Legal advice on the precise meaning of the wording of your lease is vital, because the courts have attributed subtle differences of meaning to various nuances of wording.

It is often worthwhile having a surveyor inspect the premises and advise you before you complete the negotiations to purchase the business. His report will ensure that you are not caught out by some unpleasant surprises and it will probably give you some additional ammunition in negotiations with the vendor.

Rent reviews

When a lease comes to an end, a landlord will normally offer a new one to the existing tenant, usually at a higher rent. If you feel he is asking too much money, you can apply to the court for an adjudication but you will need to take professional advice on this. Should you be unwilling to pay the figure adjudicated, you must vacate the premises. The rent is decided upon the basis of market value. You cannot expect a lower figure as one can when a 'fair rent' is fixed for domestic accommodation.

An existing tenant is normally well placed to negotiate a small discount from the market rental because of the expense to the landlord of finding a new occupant and the risk of the premises being unoccupied.

Sometimes a lease makes provision for rent reviews every few years. It might be for 15 years with a review every five years. Such a review is merely an opportunity for the landlord to raise the rent and, provided you have met your obligations as a tenant, it does not allow him to terminate the lease.

Options to buy the freehold

Sometimes an option to buy the freehold of a property can be negotiated as part of the lease. If possible, you should have a fixed value placed on this but usually no figure is stated, this being a matter for adjudication in the case of disagreement. Such an option can be helpful because a sitting tenant will normally be able to buy at a discount from the open market value of the premises when empty. One reason is that few people want to invest in small shops which are already let. The risks are high and the management troublesome, so the investment value is lower than the price when vacant possession is available. Thus a tenant can profit by buying at the lower value resulting from his occupation and reselling the business plus property.

Questions on Chapter 7

1. Have you read the lease? You — not just your solicitor.

2. If there is no lease but rent is being paid, do you realise that the landlord may be able to give you notice to quit at any time and with little compensation?

3. How long is the lease? Does it give you an option to renew it, and does it provide for periodic rent reviews?

4. Do you know the five reasons a landlord can refuse to renew a lease under the Landlord and Tenant Act?

5. If the lease has only a few years to run, is the landlord likely to renew it? If there is doubt about this, does the rent reflect it?

6. Do you realise that, should you wish to improve or replace the shop front, you can only obtain compensation for the value of this work if the landlord refuses to renew the lease and you obtained his consent before doing the work?

7. Could the business readily be moved to another site if necessary?

8. Does the lease give you the following rights:
   (a) to use the premises preferably as you wish but at least for all existing purposes and any you contemplate?
   (b) to transfer the lease to anyone you please, subject only to satisfactory references? ie the landlord may not unreasonably withhold his consent.

9. What are the tenant's repair obligations under the lease?

10. Is there an obligation to redecorate either inside or outside the premises at fixed intervals? Has it been complied with in the past? What is the likely cost of doing it next time, and when is it due to be done?

11. Is there a backlog of general repairs to the premises which has so far been ignored by the landlord but which the tenant will be responsible for, as and when the landlord chooses to enforce the terms of the lease?

12. Has the landlord complied with his own repair obligations?

13. Have you considered having a surveyor's report on the property in the light of the respective repair obligations of the landlord and the tenant under the lease?

14. If the lease has only a few years to run, will the landlord replace it now with another for a longer period? The higher rent payable might be justified by the greater security of tenure.

Chapter 8
Judging the Price – How Does One Value a Business?

The price which a business will fetch depends mostly on how keen the vendor is to sell and how anxious the purchaser is to buy. This is a matter of horsetrading, just as it is when buying and selling many secondhand items. There is no such thing as an exact valuation which holds for all purposes or in all circumstances. It depends on so many different factors. If you compare two apparently similar businesses, one may have serious flaws which make it expensive, compared to the other.

Freehold property

The value of freehold property can vary greatly according to its condition and location. The living accommodation in a modern building in one part of the city may be worth thousands of pounds more than that in an older house in another less favoured area. This commonplace of the residential market applies also to business property.

A building society survey is a valuation only on behalf of the society, not you. It provides no guarantee as to the condition of the building. You are more likely to be trying to obtain a bank or finance house mortgage, but the same applies to any survey made on behalf of a lender. Ask for details by all means but do not rely on them entirely.

Leashold property

The comments on repair obligations in the previous section on leases are very important.

Surveys

There are three kinds of survey which you can commission yourself. A *valuation survey* is primarily concerned with value; a *standard structural survey* includes an inspection of the fabric of the building; only a *full structural survey* includes hidden timbers, electric wiring, plumbing and drains and can therefore be considered a thorough review of the property.

Such a survey might also take into account work needed to bring the premises up to the requirements of the local Environmental Health, Fire and Planning Officers, any one of whom may be entitled to insist on changes. Do not imagine that all the current requirements have been met, merely because the authorities never told the previous owner to do anything.

The vendor's accounts

Strictly speaking, you are only entitled to see the profit and loss account of the vendor, not his balance sheet. The balance sheet will show what he paid for the business and this is information to which you are not entitled. However, if he shows you his full accounts, there is no reason why you should not take advantage of this. If you know that he bought the business only a year or two ago, the information about what he paid for it could be most useful in your negotiations with him.

When considering the profits of the business, which will be available to you, be sure to make adjustments for such items as motor expenses. And have all the rates, electricity and telephone bills been charged to the business, or has some part already been included in his drawings as private? See the comments in Chapter 3.

The interest charges will reflect his borrowings, not yours, and you should take these out and substitute your own. Remember that the interest only is chargeable for tax purposes. The capital repayments must be made out of post-tax income.

Goodwill

'Goodwill' is a heading which often appears in a balance sheet. What it means there is the excess of the price paid by the owner of the business over the value of the assets he bought. It is a book entry only, not something you can touch and it is *not* some magical value resulting from the reputation of the business.

When you are buying a business you will often find a vendor talking of his goodwill as worth 'so many times net profit'. In isolation from the rest of the calculations this is economic nonsense. You may have to disabuse your prospective vendor of this fiction yourself before he will talk sense about the price he wants.

People are often confused about goodwill. Goodwill is *not an identifiable asset* with its own value. It is in effect a balancing figure arrived at as follows.

Say you are offered a business earning a net profit of £8000. You are prepared to pay one and a half years' profits for it, plus stock at valuation. You are therefore buying the leasehold, fixed assets and goodwill for £12,000. If the equipment, fixtures and fittings are valued at £7000 you are paying £5000 for the right to the leasehold (not usually separated from goodwill) and the goodwill. If any debtors or creditors were taken over, they would be a part of the calculation.

However, this is a half truth. The value of the assets always depends upon the view you take of them. If you value them for use as they stand in a going concern, they are worth far more than if you tried to sell them off as surplus. So the balancing figure taken as the value of goodwill is arbitrary. One cannot value goodwill for itself − only as a consequence of deciding what one will pay for a given amount of profit and then deducting one's valuation of the assets from the price paid.

How high is the price being asked?

After taking out an estimate of the value of the property, how many years' purchase of the pre-tax profits does the balance of the price represent? Many small businesses sell on around one to one-and-a-half years' purchase of the profits, though the figure tends to be higher in the south of England.

If you are paying £36,000 for a business which is earning pre-tax profits of £12,000, you are buying it on three years' purchase. This is equivalent to a return on your money of $33^1/3$ per cent before tax. If it costs you 17 per cent to borrow the money, a $33^1/3$ per cent return is as low as it is sensible to accept. Businesses often sell at, say, one-and-a-half years' purchase, a return of $66^2/3$ per cent, but because this ignores your salary it is not a true return. If you could earn £200 per week working for someone else and your business is earning £12,000, you have only true profits of £1600 after deducting your salary. This represents the real return. So, if you paid £18,000, ie only one-and-a-half years' pre-tax profits, you would really be earning about 9 per cent on your money, ie £1600 on £18,000.

What are the real profits?

Watch out for sales increasing rapidly in the year or two before the business is put up for sale. This could mean that the figures are being dressed up in some way, possibly by the inclusion of takings which were previously concealed, or possibly by lowering prices to stimulate business in the short term. The latter should show up in lower profits, but this can sometimes be concealed by boosting the stock valuation.

If the vendor claims extra hidden profits not declared, you should remind yourself that he has been cheating and that there is a serious risk of being caught out, not only for income tax, but also for VAT. The morality of not declaring takings is a matter for you and the vendor; very often the figures are not all that large in relation to the profits. Nevertheless, one can argue that, if he has not declared the sales, the vendor should not obtain the value in his selling price. You yourself will run serious risks of severe VAT and tax penalties if you continue the practice.

In the end, any alleged 'true' sales are merely a point to be taken into account in the negotiations, since it is really a question of how much you are prepared to pay and how much he will accept. But always be suspicious of anyone who claims to have concealed a significant part of their profits. If they are willing to admit such a deception to you in order to persuade you to buy the business, what other bits of chicanery are going on, about which you are not being told?

If you can see accounts for two or three years, you will have a pattern of results of the business. Sometimes, however, up-to-date accounts are not available and unaudited figures may only be available for a short period. This can happen when a business has recently changed hands and is being resold. Beware of this, since the figures may not be representative of the annual results and may show short-term trends only. Check also whether VAT has been eliminated.

Checking the claimed sales figure

If you look through the purchase invoices for the business for a period, you should get a fair idea of whether the claimed sales are correct. This is very simple in some cases where few main items are sold, eg a fish and chip shop. You can check quantities bought each week and, since stocks will be small, you can compare the claimed sales with the purchase totals. Even for something more complicated, like a grocery and general store, you will often find that there is only a limited number of main suppliers' invoices which will account for the bulk of the sales; much useful information can be gleaned by going through them.

Do the gross profit and stock figures make sense?

Business ratios are explained in detail in *Understanding Your Accounts* by A St J Price (Kogan Page, 1986). You should check that gross profit ratio in the accounts to see how it compares with the normal figure for that type of shop. There can be many reasons, connected with buying and pricing policy, which affect this. Make sure you understand how they apply in this case. Similarly the stock ratio gives you clues as to how well the shop is managed, whether there is overstocking, and so on.

Wholesale sales

Sometimes one finds a business which is doing a proportion of its sales at wholesale rates to other businesses; a baker, who bakes for a couple of other shops, as well as for his own, is a possible example. These sales will be at much lower profit margins and this must be taken into account.

Personal 'franchise' of the owner

If the vendor has been in business for a long time in his area, people may come to him because of his personality etc. Whether this matters very much depends on the nature of the business but in some cases his knowledge is a critical factor in the profits which he has made. A newcomer will not be able to do as well under any circumstances.

The owner should agree to introduce you to the business and to the customers for, say, a couple of weeks either immediately before or just after you take over. He should also contract not to set up in competition for a reasonable period and within a reasonable distance, but usually these conditions are not very restricting. The courts will not prevent a man from earning his living and in a city a time limit of, say, two years and a distance of perhaps a mile might be all that would be enforceable in law.

Seeing through the sales blurb

Several of the questions at the end of this chapter deal with points about the so-called 'potential' of the business. This is a favourite phrase employed by agents and it needs to be treated with great suspicion. What it often means is that, if you are prepared to work a 12-hour day, seven days a week, you will increase the sales. The fact that you will probably kill yourself in the process is not mentioned. Is the potential there? Was the business mismanaged? Are changes due shortly in the neighbourhood, eg big new housing developments?

What about existing equipment and fittings?

Look hard at these. Do all the items work? Are they going to be satisfactory for your purpose or will you have to replace them? If you do have to sell them, you will find they fetch a fraction of their replacement cost. A business which has old equipment is not worth nearly as much as one which is well fitted out. Yet the values attributed may well be similar and it is up to you to see the difference and to negotiate accordingly.

Incidentally, you should check the ownership of all the items. If any of them are on hire purchase, the vendor must pay this up in full before he can sell them to you. Other items may be rented or leased and are therefore not available for sale to you. You may be able to take over the leasing or rental agreements, but you should not include anything in the valuation when considering the price you are being asked to pay.

Existing staff

Do you want to take on all the existing staff or not? If not, you should negotiate this as part of the deal because, once you take over the business, you also take over the contract of employment of anybody who works for it. You then become responsible for any redundancy payments.

Questions on Chapter 8

1. If freehold property is included, have you taken professional advice on
   (a) its value?
   (b) its condition? A preliminary inspection may suggest that a detailed survey is needed.

2. Do you understand the difference between a
   (a) valuation survey — primarily concerned with value
   (b) standard structural survey — inspects fabric of
       building
   (c) full structural survey — includes hidden timbers,
       electric wiring, plumbing and drains?

3. Have you taken professional advice (or checked with the
   local Environmental Health, Fire and Planning Officers)
   on work needed to bring the premises up to the standard
   required by the various regulations?

4. Have you seen the vendor's accounts as prepared for tax
   purposes? (You are only entitled to see his profit and loss
   account, not the balance sheet.)

5. What are the profits of the business (before tax and
   drawings)? Have you adjusted for
   (a) items, such as motor expenses, which are really
       private?
   (b) interest on money borrowed by the vendor? (Your
       borrowings will be different from his and your own
       interest will be allowed for separately.)

6. How many years' profits does the price of the business
   represent? Is this normal for the area and the trade? Do
   you understand the explanation of goodwill and what it
   really means?

7. How do the profits compare with what you can earn in a
   job after allowing for tax benefits?

8. How secure are the profits and what has been their trend
   over the last three years?

9. Have profits been boosted artificially in anticipation of a
   sale
   (a) by including sales previously undeclared?
   (b) by long hours/cut prices/heavy advertising?

10. Does the vendor claim extra hidden profit not shown in
    the accounts?

11. Are you satisfied that the sales figures quoted to you are
    realistic, not wishful thinking or based on short periods
    unrepresentative of the full year? Has VAT been taken
    out of them?

12. Do sales include any deals or contracts in bulk at wholesale prices and therefore at lower profit margins?

13. Does the present owner have a personal 'franchise' on the trade due to length of time established, local reputation, particular knowledge or skill? You must expect to lose some trade initially when you take over a good business, but could it be unusually hard for you to match the previous owner's reputation and pulling power?

14. Will the owner
    (a) agree to introduce you into the business and to the customers for a couple of weeks or so?
    (b) contract not to set up in competition for a reasonable period and within a reasonable distance?

15. Is there scope to develop the trade? Is this real or is it part of the sales blurb of the agent?

16. If the scope is real, do you believe the vendor's explanation as to why he has not exploited it himself?

17. Is he a good, average or poor shopkeeper himself?

18. Have you checked the stated sales by reference to the vendor's purchase invoices from his suppliers? If he is buying regularly, he is probably selling through the shop, unless he has an outlet elsewhere.

19. What is the value of the equipment, fixtures and fittings? Expensive shop fittings, once installed, are only worth a good proportion of their cost for so long as they draw trade and serve a purpose in that shop. Have you assessed realistically their value at auction or to a dealer, if you have to change them?

20. Are any items being leased or rented by the vendor? If so, a change of contract is needed and you should check the terms. An HP agreement must be settled in full by the vendor before he can sell you the items.

21. Is the equipment up-to-date and does it work?

22. Has the equipment been properly maintained?

23. Do any of the fixtures and fittings and equipment need immediate replacement
    (a) because they do not meet statutory regulations?

(b) because they are of poor quality, inefficient, out of date etc?

This applies particularly to specialised businesses such as launderettes.

24. Could your spouse run the business, while you go on working, until the shop can support you both? Is he or she strong enough
   (a) physically — moving stock, long hours etc?
   (b) mentally — stress of responsibility, bookwork, handling money etc?

25. Is there a potential liability for redundancy pay to staff employed by the vendor for many years? Do you need them? Should you dismiss them now or later?

Chapter 9

Negotiating the Deal – Have You Done Your Homework?

I had no idea how much most people hate haggling until I started in the business of selling shops. Negotiating a deal does not come naturally to British people. All too often a purchase is not really negotiated at all. This means that if you do your homework on the deal and if you then apply some simple principles, you will put yourself at a considerable advantage over most vendors.

The first problem is that most people, for obvious reasons, do not have enough practice in negotiating big deals. Nevertheless, this is not an exercise to be frightened of. Here are some points which will help you.

First you should realise that a good negotiator divides the process into three distinct stages. These are as follows:

1. The information-gathering stage
2. The 'What is the deal?' stage
3. Closing the deal.

If you skip either of the first two stages, you are negotiating with one hand tied behind your back. You have seriously handicapped yourself and have thus reduced your chances of obtaining the best possible deal.

The information-gathering stage

This is your first visit to the shop when you view the premises and find out as much as you can about the way it trades, what it sells, how much it sells, the terms of any lease, past profits etc. You should also try to find out why the vendor wants to sell. This can be very important. Are his stated reasons the real ones and can you exploit them to your advantage?

The 'What is the deal?' stage

Here the problem is to find out precisely what the vendor is prepared to offer. You should *not* yet have made a bid. You are merely clarifying his asking price. (The agent's particulars may quote a figure, but when you actually ask the vendor how much he wants, he may give you a different, lower figure or he may indicate that the one quoted is 'negotiable'.) Either way, you have won an immediate point, while conceding nothing yourself. You have established that you can definitely do a deal at a lower figure and the third stage will be a question of how much. Meanwhile, you are still not making an offer — you are trying to find out what associated terms the vendor is prepared to give you 'on a plate', ie without your having to negotiate for them. The vendor may well be prepared to make various concessions which are not related to the actual price, but which are nevertheless worth money to you. For example, he may offer to work with you in the business, preferably before you take it over, for perhaps a couple of weeks. Another is the question of stocks. Normally he will want you to take over everything in the shop but, particularly with some specialist items, it is always possible that he will be prepared to take these with him. Perhaps he would accept a delayed payment for the business, say 50 per cent down and the balance over a year or even longer, or maybe he will take with him items of equipment which you do not want, thus reducing the price.

In practice there is limited scope for such concessions in the sale of a small shop, but it is always worth looking for them. Remember that at this stage you are still *not negotiating*. You are simply asking him exactly what the deal is which he is prepared to offer you. Obviously you are interested or you would not be asking the questions.

Ideally you should make three visits to the premises, each visit being a separate stage. Of course, this is not always practicable — there may be other parties on the point of making an offer.

I think it is impossible to make the best deal after a single visit, even if you go through the three stages as distinct processes. You are making an instant decision if you make an offer on your first visit, and this is not advisable.

A second visit is always invaluable because of the things you will spot which you did not notice on your first visit. You will be astonished at how unobservant you appear to have been. Partly, of course, this is the result of some natural excitement at seeing a place which might be suitable. The first time round, inevitably, you will tend to see the good points rather than the bad and to have 'stars in your eyes'.

Choosing a business is a very important decision which requires careful consideration and a second look, at least.

Closing the deal

It is a standard ploy for a vendor to suggest that he has other people about to make an offer. This may well be true, but try probing a little further. Ask when the vendor expects to receive their offer. Have they cash in the bank, or does he think they will have to borrow? Are they people already in the same trade or is this their first venture?

These questions may appear rather direct in cold print but you can make them less so in conversation. If there is substance to the vendor's claim, the answers will probably make this apparent; if he has invented the other people or is merely indulging in wishful thinking, this should also become apparent. It is legitimate for you to ask what time limit there may be during which he expects to have to make a decision. *Never* allow yourself to be pushed into making an offer there and then on the grounds that he expects to hear from the others tomorrow. If a vendor is serious about the possibility of your buying the business, he will give you a day or two to come up with a better figure. If he tries to rush you and you call his bluff, you have at once put yourself in a stronger position. You can then take your time and reduce your offer accordingly.

All of this may sound a little complicated but it really comes down to common sense and taking your time, rather than rushing in where angels fear to tread.

Remember that there is no one 'right' price for any business. A good agent will know roughly what he expects it to fetch, based on the prices of similar businesses sold recently, but a determined buyer or a determined seller may well swing the price of a particular deal by a substantial margin. In other words, it all depends on who wants to do a deal the most — the buyer or the seller.

When you first start looking seriously at businesses and you think that you have found the right one, the temptation is to assume this is the only business for you. In fact, this is almost never the case and there is always another just around the corner. So do try to avoid too much emotional involvement in any particular deal. If you can decide on the right price and then be fairly cold-blooded about negotiating that figure, you stand a much better chance of achieving it. If you go into negotiations with the feeling that you *must* have this business, you are almost certainly going to have to pay more for it. That is the market-place at work! This is where taking a second or a third look at the premises helps so much. The scales drop away from your eyes and you find it much easier to see it for what it really is — a reasonable proposition in most cases, provided that you can buy it at the right price.

Of course, there are exceptional opportunities which occasionally crop up. Perhaps you have known the business for some time and already done a great deal of homework and are therefore sure of your choice. This is fine but remember the three stages of negotiation — compress them as much as you dare. Remember, too, that there are many businesses which look better than they really are, and few whose attractions need seeking out.

Are you clear why you want the business?

The questions at the end of the chapter note some points. If none of them applies, you should have two or three other good ones, or this is not the business for you.

All that glitters is not gold

I have said it before, and I must say it again — very few businesses offer good money for short hours and no previous experience. If you think you are on to such a chance, you are probably blind to the problems. You should do all you can to check with others more knowledgeable than yourself. The economics are obvious; if it were that easy, everyone else would jump in for a killing and the rule of the market-place would promptly bring the profits back to a more reasonable level.

Watch out for compliments

Do not let yourself be taken in by flattery from the vendor. When it comes to money, people are usually realistic; it is of no interest to them whether or not they like the purchaser and you should treat with the greatest suspicion remarks such as 'I'd like to do a deal with you' or 'You're obviously a good negotiator'. The latter should put you on your guard against being taken in by some piece of flannel.

Avoid ultimatums

If you issue an ultimatum to the vendor such as 'I must have an answer by tomorrow' this may work, but it also forces the situation. If the vendor fails to respond, what do you do? If you go back to him, you have shown him that your ultimatum was hollow and you have weakened your position.

On the other hand, you may be able to turn an ultimatum issued *to you* by the vendor to your advantage. More often than not you can ignore it and thus weaken his position. Sometimes a vendor will send out contracts to two different buyers promising to deal with the first one who signs up. If you desperately want the business, you will respond but if you can look at the deal dispassionately, this is an excellent opportunity to improve your negotiating position. In such cases the other prospective purchaser often fails to proceed for one reason or another. If he does not buy, the vendor will have to come back to you. This is your opportunity to make a fresh offer at a lower price, knowing that the competition has withdrawn and that the vendor will now be wondering whether he is going to get a deal at all.

If you reject an ultimatum, do so by not replying to it. The vendor will then have to come back to you for an answer.

Making an actual offer

When you do make your offer, it should lie 'on the table' until the vendor makes a counter proposition. For instance, if his asking price is £30,000 and you offer £25,000, you *must* wait for him to respond by a lower figure on his side before you up yours. This assumes that your figure was a serious one in the first place; you made it because you thought the business was overpriced or because you were sure this was a weak seller. In either case you should await developments, prepared to justify your figure with as many arguments as you can produce as to why it is more reasonable than his. In other words, keep talking, but do not raise your figure and be prepared to get up and walk out if necessary. You can always say something like, 'Well, that is the figure I think is fair and I have tried to explain why. Perhaps you would like to sleep on it and we can talk again in the morning.'

Alternatively, when he has himself produced arguments of some possible weight, you can agree to consider what he has said. Either way, you leave him in suspense and with the feeling

71

that while there is a deal to be done, he is not going to get it at his original level.

Even if you feel there is no time to lose in concluding the matter, there is nothing to be lost by sitting around and twiddling your thumbs for a while. It may be dangerous to change the topic of conversation because this will distract the attention of the vendor from the points you have been trying to make. You can always say something like, 'Would you like a few minutes to think over what we have discussed?'

If he has made some apparently cogent points which seem to have knocked holes in your own arguments, you can always try a minute or two's silence yourself, interrupted by an occasional 'Oh' or 'I see', indicating that you are allowing what he has said to sink in. This may encourage him to press home an apparent advantage by volunteering a small reduction in the hope of tempting you into a deal.

These various tactical points are merely to start you thinking. Perhaps you know of better ways to negotiate yourself. The point is that a well-conducted campaign of this kind will crack the defences of all but the most determined vendor who has no intention whatever of selling at anything but the price originally quoted. If this is the case, there is no need for unpleasantness. Once you have established that this really is so, you have a choice: to pay or not to pay. This will depend on your judgement of whether or not it is fair. There is nothing unfair about your having tried to reduce what you thought to be a reasonable price in the first place; that is just the market-place in operation.

Marshalling your arguments

As part of the negotiating process, you should assemble a list of points which you can use to press home the point that the business is not worth as much as the owner is asking for it. List any defects which you have noticed in the property, disadvantages inherent in the lease (see the chapter on leases pages 51-5), state of the equipment and fittings. Even though they may not be of great significance individually, when listed and thrown at the other side one after the other the general effect can be quite impressive. It takes a resolute vendor not to crumble, at least a little, in the face of a concerted attack. I make no excuse for using the terminology of a battle — this is what it is to some extent and you are entitled to probe his defences with every means at your disposal.

Take outside advice

I have a vested interest in suggesting that professional help could be useful to you. Unfortunately, there are few accountants or solicitors who have much experience of negotiating themselves and you may find it difficult to get help from them with the actual bargaining. But at least you should discuss the deal with them and go through it for possible disadvantages.

I have found, in each of the negotiations in which I have been retained by the purchaser to help him, that my services have more than paid for themselves in terms of reductions negotiated in the price. Sometimes my advice is not to do the deal at all but I am probably saving the purchaser a great deal of money which he would have lost had he gone ahead.

Who can give you good advice? Do not ask your best friend. Well-intentioned people accompanying you can spoil the deal by failing to keep their mouths shut at the right moment, or interjecting remarks which you have purposely avoided making for tactical reasons. Perhaps you know a businessman who has done more than one deal himself and whose judgement you trust. Alternatively your accountant or solicitor, attending as a silent observer, may be a great help with comments made in the intervals between negotiating when you 'go outside'.

Even though such professionals may know comparatively little about the realities of small businesses, their background knowledge and experience can be valuable. An impartial observer may well spot points which you have missed. Also, if the vendor is on his own, you have the psychological advantage of two people against one.

The role of the vendor's agent

One person to whom you must never go for advice is the business transfer agent acting for the vendors. Do get your thinking straight on this point. You are entitled to rely on the accuracy of statements of fact made by him, but on nothing else. After all, are you paying his fees or is the vendor? You cannot expect him to tell you whether the business is reasonably priced or whether it is the right buy for you. Indeed, he could be failing to fulfil his duty to his client should he say anything to you on this subject, other than to make remarks aimed at boosting the value of the business in your eyes.

Subject to contract

This is an important legal phrase governing the basis on which you pay a deposit. You should never pay one to the vendor himself, but always to his solicitor or to the business transfer agent acting for him. Ten per cent of the purchase price is normal and the phrase 'subject to contract' ensures that this is a returnable sum, should you decide not to sign the contract *for any reason*.

This means that you can change your mind right up to the stage where you sign. The point is that, in making payment of an initial sum, you have given evidence of good faith. People do not normally pay deposits, unless, at that stage, they seriously intend to go through with the deal, and it will normally stop the vendor dealing with any other possible buyer.

Incidentally, there are two stages to completing the deal. The first is to sign and exchange contracts between the solicitors acting for the two parties; the second is to 'complete' the transaction by handing over the property and assets against payment. The latter stage takes place on a date to be mutually agreed and it may be a matter of days, weeks, and sometimes months, after signature of the contract.

Beware of the 'auction'

Just as during a boom in house prices, buyers may find themselves being 'gazumped', so may you. Gazumping means the owner agreeing a deal with one purchaser and then using that as a bargaining counter with the next person. If he finds someone else prepared to up the price before the contract with the first purchaser is signed, he cancels the first deal. Since it usually takes six to twelve weeks for the two firms of solicitors to clear the various searches and other formalities and to get the contract ready for signature, sellers quite often receive better offers in the interim when demand for businesses is good and prices are rising.

There is little which you can do to protect yourself from this. Paying a deposit 'subject to contract' commits no one and is merely evidence of your good faith and that you have the necessary money available. Either you or the other side can withdraw, simply by taking exception to the terms of the contract.

It is unwise to pay a deposit without this reservation, since, though you may be able thereby to get a written commitment from the seller to part with his business, you will also be tying yourself into what may prove on reflection and on investigation by a solicitor to be a lousy deal.

Buying a business is, after all, purely a matter of business, and the best advice I can give you is to be 'tough' about it. As soon as you agree a deal, you will start to incur expenses such as a solicitor's fees in preparing a contract, preparations to move, leave your job and so on, but it is no use worrying too much about this. If the deal is going to go sour, or you lose it because someone else is prepared to pay more, it is better to accept the situation rather than chase the price up above a sensible figure. If you have agreed what you believe to be the top price you can prudently pay, stop there. It is always possible that you will get the business after all. The following story explains why.

Occasionally, the seller of the business, and his agent, are faced with two keen buyers at once. The same evening that I advertised one business I received a telephone call from a man who recognised it from its description and had wished to buy it for some time. He committed himself straight away to pay the asking price and promised to forward a deposit. Naturally I was pleased, but I am always a little suspicious of rapid deals. I prefer a buyer to have thought about things at least overnight. People who make instant decisions of this magnitude tend to reflect more soberly in due course or are brought to their senses by their advisers. Perhaps they may even read this book! They then back off, leaving the owner and his agent with the problem of re-advertising or having to approach other more serious buyers with the disadvantage of one deal having already fallen through.

In this case, I was not able to contact the owner that night and the following morning, before I could do so, he rang me. 'I've sold the business,' were his first words. 'Yes, I know,' I replied. 'Mr B rang me last night...'. 'No, it's a Mr and Mrs J,' was the reply.

Oh dear! I had accepted one offer and the owner another, both at the asking price. We could hardly be blamed for the situation but this was small consolation to either of the two buyers. Each maintained that he should have priority, one because he got in first and the other because he saw the shop at the earliest possible moment after he had received the particulars. It was unfair that the other individual had seen the premises before receiving the details.

There was no way I could satisfy both potential buyers but, anyway, my prime responsibility was to my client, the vendor. I

75

was unhappy about the whole situation, feeling it to be unsound that two people were taking such instant decisions to buy. After discussing the matter with my client, we agreed to send out draft contracts to both people and to conclude a deal with the first party, who was ready to sign. This was a way of putting some pressure on both of them not to muck about without actually having an 'auction' to see who would bid the highest.

We could have invited bids from the pair of them, perhaps doing it on the basis of a sealed envelope being deposited by a given date with the vendor's solicitors. This is sometimes done but both it and contract 'races' are dangerous practices for the seller. They can rebound badly.

In every deal, whether to buy a house, a business or whatever, the buyer has an initial moment of enthusiasm, usually followed by a cooling off period in which he sees some of the cons as well as the pros and during which he takes a more dispassionate view of what he originally saw as a bargain and just the very property for him. You are unlikely to make a good decision unless you go through the process ending up still convinced, having cooled off, that the pros of a deal outweigh the cons.

As the agent in this particular one, I was unhappy because I felt that both buyers might change their minds after they had had more time to think the matter through properly and I had visions of us ending up with no deal in consequence. It was thus rather against my better judgement that I accepted the idea of a contract race. Incidentally, these are disliked by many solicitors and agents on both sides of the deal, partly for the above reasons and partly because it puts on the pressure for further rushed decisions. It also involves potential buyers in some expense with no certainty that they will be able to proceed.

I have explained all this in detail because you might find yourself in this position as a buyer and you should understand the various considerations. In the event one buyer did indeed cool off and did not submit a signed contract; fortunately the other proceeded. Had he realised that his competitor had with-drawn and, especially if he himself had begun to have any doubts about the price, he would have been in a strong position to withdraw his original offer and make a lower bid, knowing that we might very well accept a reduction of several hundred pounds rather than suffer the additional expense and delay of re-advertising.

If you find yourself competing for a business, my advice is to sit on your hands for a while. It is unlikely that this is so perfect a proposition for you that you cannot find a sequel elsewhere; should your competitor not proceed for one reason or the other, you are then well placed to negotiate a favourable deal. Incidentally, do not reply to an invitation to engage in a race, or to bid above the original asking price. Say nothing and make the vendor come back to you for an answer. That way, you will know that he is still interested in your enquiry and has probably been unable to do a satisfactory deal elsewhere.

Questions on Chapter 9

1. Why are you buying this business? What advantages does it offer you? Here are some possible ones:
   (a) A chance to learn the trade and gain experience at minimum risk. The price is low and within your resources. The lock-up shop is close to home so you have no removal costs etc.
   (b) A good trading opportunity. There is space to expand the business. Trade is growing nationally or locally. The vendor is a poor shopkeeper etc.
   (c) The business offers a secure and adequate income in a pleasant area suitable for retirement.
   (d) The business offers your wife/husband a good income without too much strain on your family life.

2. Could you be making the common mistake of underrating the skill/knowledge/experience required? No trade is ever as simple as it looks.

3. Do you realise that in most cases the 'other people interested' are no nearer to a decision than you, if indeed they are serious at all, and that more often than not an offer below the asking price and/or a request for reasonable time to think over the deal will not lose you the opportunity of buying?

4. Do you know that more bad decisions to buy than good ones are made in a hurry, and that there are usually a couple of other sound businesses available elsewhere which are equally suitable?

5. Do you understand the importance of being willing to 'sit around a bit' when negotiating?

6. Do you understand the term 'subject to contract'? Have you considered whether your offer should also be subject to some other matter such as the transfer of a lease, grant of a sub postmastership etc?

7. Did you see the business and meet the proprietor at least twice before making an offer?

8. The second time did you take an experienced friend or professional adviser with you to help you ask the right questions?

9. Have your wife and family seen and liked both the business and the area?

10. Have you taken advice on the deal from an independent accountant or business transfer agent, preferably based on an inspection of the business?

11. Have you quoted to the vendor any defects in the property revealed by a survey, if you have had one done?

12. Do you understand that the vendor's agents and advisers, being paid by him, are under contract to him to try to obtain the best possible price?

13. If asked for a deposit of 10 per cent to show that you are a serious buyer do you know that you should pay this either to the vendor's solicitor or to the business transfer agent acting for him and *not* to the vendor himself? And that it should be paid 'subject to contract'?

14. Do you realise that it is the contract, not the payment of a deposit, which gives you a legal right (and obligation) to buy? It is possible to make a preliminary contract accompanied by a deposit, but the vendor is likely to demand that the deposit be non-returnable and the risk to the purchaser is not normally justified by his need to be sure of the deal.

15. If buying a leasehold, have you enquired as to the possibility of an option to buy the freehold at a later date? Sometimes this can be obtained. Provided that no payment is made for it, it can be useful.

16. When fixing a target date for takeover have you allowed adequate time for the following:
(a) Legal searches etc? If a particular district is in arrears

the authorities may take some weeks to reply to your solicitor.

(b) Surveys required by you or by those lending to you?

(c) Completion of formalities by any lender to you?

(d) Sale of your own house if applicable? The above points apply to that deal as well, although bridging finance from your bank may be available to you.

(e) Agreement of landlord to transfer of lease to you or grant of a new one to you if applicable?

(f) Approval of postmaster if buying a sub post office?

If cash is available and there are no complications, it is possible to complete a deal within a month, but this is unusual. Most take two to three months from initial agreement on price etc to the actual handover.

17. Before agreeing the deal have you insisted on a list of fixtures, fittings and equipment? Have you checked that the major items are in working order, are owned not rented or leased, and are not the landlord's property? Exterior sun blinds, for example, once fitted to the shop front become the landlord's fixtures.

Chapter 10

Takeover Checklist – What about these Points?

As the date on which you take over your new venture approaches, you will be very busy. You will have a lot on your mind with arrangements to leave your job, move house etc. It is easy to forget important points which should be dealt with before the day. Here is a list. Some can be coped with beforehand but others arise on the actual day and the list should help you to make sure that nothing is overlooked.

It is easier to find time to see people, visit other shops, exhibitions, showrooms etc before you take over than it is once you are involved in the daily routine of your own business. You should consider leaving your existing job a month or two beforehand so as to give you time. It will pay you to make good use of this period in talking to others in the trade, meeting your future suppliers, and so on.

What will the vendor do about stocks?

Is he to carry on reordering as usual, or do you want him to reduce the quantities of goods held to the minimum? There is a limit to which this can be done without losing goodwill as a result of items being out of stock. But taking over low stocks means a smaller lump sum of cash for you to pay. You will then have whatever credit period your suppliers will give you before you have to pay for the goods which you buy in. Of course, if you deal with a cash and carry wholesaler, this does not apply. However, you do have the freedom to buy in the goods which you want, rather than those the vendor has chosen.

This advantage can be illusory since, if this is your first business, the vendor will know much more about what sells than you do. Another point is that it tends to be the quick selling lines which are cleared, not the slow-moving ones. It is the latter which you would most like to be rid of! However, low stocks do help counting on the day and reduce the problem of valuation. Usually the answer is a sensible compromise and you should discuss the point with the vendor.

Valuation of stocks

You must agree beforehand the basis on which stock is to be valued to ensure that you do not pay more for it to the vendor than he himself paid. Beware of stock which has been on hand for some time and which was therefore bought at lower prices. The vendor may argue that he is entitled to the profit resulting from the increased cost of this stock while he has held it. The answer to that one is that if he has failed to sell it, either it is slow-moving, in which case it may even be worth less than he paid, or there is too much of it. Either way he should not make a profit on selling it to you.

Often stock is taken at selling price and then reduced by a standard percentage. Yet a shop which sells, say, ladies' tights, cans of baked beans and cigarettes, has different profit margins on each. A grocery and general store will have some items on which there are margins ranging above 25 per cent to $33^1/_3$ per cent or more; probably the majority of its stock is at between 14 per cent and 20 per cent and some goods may earn less. The margin on cigarettes, for instance, is less than 10 per cent. So an overall percentage can be misleading. If it is too low, you are paying too much for the goods since the sale price will not be reduced sufficiently.

VAT on stock

If stock is valued at selling prices which include VAT, make sure that the reduction to cost is sufficient to eliminate the tax. The vendor is not entitled to charge you VAT which he recovered when he bought the goods. See also the section on value added tax on pages 85-8.

What about old stock?

Every shop has some items which are more or less unsaleable. This may be due to lack of demand, poor stock rotation, damage, obsolescence etc. Whatever the reason, you should not expect to have to buy the vendor's mistakes, though you may have to compromise by taking some items at a reduced price.

The services of an independent stocktaker are likely to be very useful, because he knows how to take stock quickly and efficiently, will do the valuations for you and because he can act as an arbitrator. Fees should be split between you and the vendor.

If you organise the stock count properly in advance, you can make it give you some information about the money tied up in different types of stock. The stocktaker will want to count simply by value, ie so many items at 50p, 45p and so on. But he will have to separate the goods at different profit margins, so you should insist on having stock lists headed with the type of item, such as cigarettes, food, hardware etc (depending upon the type of shop).

The advantage of using a stocktaker

I advise using a professional stocktaker to count and value the stock when you take it over. His fee is likely to be well justified by the time and money he saves you.

Moreover, the vendor ought to split the fee with you on the grounds that the stocktaker is there to adjudicate on values, thereby helping to avoid disputes. His experience should ensure that you do not pay more than the goods are worth. Here's a story which shows why.

I was once asked to look at a business owned by two brothers. I was somewhat suspicious of them, because they seemed a pair of 'fly' lads, whose talk was a little too smooth and who had obviously 'been around' for many years in the trade. I thought their asking price was much too high, said so, and therefore did not handle the sale.

The business did eventually sell and, some time after the takeover, I chanced by the shop and had a chat with the new owners. They were now settled in and, on the whole, were not discontented with their purchase, but they knew they had paid a high price and that they had been taken for a ride in some respects. 'You know,' they told me, 'the brothers went round the stock of greetings cards increasing the retail prices by 2 or 3p each before we arrived. Since stock was taken at retail prices and the retail profit then reduced to get to the figure which we had to pay, it cost us substantially more than it should have!' Need I say more about the value of a stocktaker?

Stock records

Perhaps you can arrange to take over the buying records kept by the vendor. Efficient purchasing requires a record of *what* has been ordered from each supplier and *when*, so that one can see readily the quantities being sold. This is important as a means of preventing overbuying.

Stock control is very important because too many goods on hand eat up cash quickly. Poor control results in a large number of decisions — each decision of little importance on its own but cumulatively the result is too much money being tied up. The only way to prevent this is good records, so that you can put the salesman on the spot when he tries to persuade you to take an extra dozen of this and a few more of that on the grounds that they are on special offer.

Incidentally, in your early months in charge, get to know the manufacturers' representatives and find out which of them you can trust. The best will advise you sensibly on what to order and will not want you to overbuy. Others will push as much stock at you as they can because this improves their own commission. So be deeply suspicious of any 'special prices', 'incentive prices' and the like.

I remember my early days in business, when I owned a small tobacconist and confectionery shop. The salesman from a leading table lighter manufacturer arrived hot-foot with the most magnificent deal. 'Just the thing for you to get your fancy goods department going,' he said. 'Our full range of a dozen table lighters at 10 per cent off, plus an extra one thrown in for free. Look at all that extra profit!' The extra profit was there all right, when one had sold all 13 lighters. But the cash from that thirteenth lighter represented the extra money. We sold two or three quite quickly. Three years later we still had five left. It was a salutary lesson in business economics for me. Let it be one for you too.

The point is that manufacturers make special offers for good commercial reasons. Perhaps they are overstocked, or business is bad, or they simply want to promote that particular part of their product range. Whatever the reason, you are not going to sell either more goods or goods of a certain type or price which you do not normally sell just because you have bought them cheaply.

Manufacturers often undertake special advertising, give you counter showcards etc which help to move the goods being promoted. Nevertheless, beware of taking the plunge until you have enough experience to make a sensible judgement on what is right for your shop.

Do not forget your insurance

You must tell your motor insurers if your vehicle will now be used for business purposes. Check with your insurance broker whether there are any special risks to your particular business. For instance, if anything goes wrong with the vehicle, a mobile catering stall is out of action. You therefore need a policy which covers you for your loss of profits, if you have an accident which is entirely the fault of the other party. The ordinary policy will replace your vehicle but meanwhile where is the business?

Do you realise that you are at risk on the property from the date on which you sign the contract of purchase, not that on which you actually take it over?

Your life assurance cover

If you have left a job with a good pension scheme, you will lose valuable cover. Even if you cannot afford to replace this until the business is making better profits, you can and should buy temporary life cover which is cheap. This insures your life for 12 months at a time. There is no continuing value after the 12 months but, should you die during the period, there would be a capital sum to rescue your family from the inevitable financial strains. Consult your insurance broker.

Value added tax

VAT causes much woe to people who buy existing businesses because they do not understand that no tax ought to be charged to them on the purchase price. All too often, professional advisers such as solicitors and accountants do not know the law either and the result is a nasty shock for the purchaser later, when he finds that he cannot recover as input tax the VAT he has paid.

Many vendors think that they ought to charge VAT on either the entire price of the business or on the stock and/or equipment, which they sell as part of it. That is not so. VAT law provides that the sale of a business as a going concern is outside the scope of VAT. It is therefore illegal to charge VAT on any part of the sale price.

The same applies to a part of a business, such as one out of a chain of shops, which is capable of separate operation on its own. The only exception is if the purchaser does not immediately register for VAT — but he nearly always most do so, see page 86.

Unfortunately some vendors see charging VAT to the purchaser as a way of getting their hands on a substantial additional sum with which to pay their creditors. Sometimes a vendor just makes off with it before Customs and Excise can catch up with him. The problem is then that Customs find that they have not been paid the output tax charged by the vendor so they disallow the input tax paid and reclaimed by the purchaser. It makes no difference whether you have a proper tax invoice showing all the correct details. If the sale was outside the scope of the VAT, that's it. Customs will collect the money from you and there is nothing you can do about it!

There have been many appeals to the VAT tribunals on this subject by aggrieved purchasers who have lost money. Customs usually win but that does not mean that interpreting the legal provisions in relation to an individual situation is easy. It can be complicated. However, the sale of a shop while it is trading is usually clear cut as the transfer of a going concern and no VAT should be added. If the vendor insists that it should be, consult your professional advisers and ask them to look up the law in the VAT Special Provisions Order. If still unable to resolve the matter to your satisfaction, insist on going with the vendor to Customs to discuss the matter and obtain a ruling from them. Do not submit to pressure from the vendor. The more insistent he is, the more likely it is that there is something wrong. You can always pay the extra VAT to your solicitor to be held pending agreement on the matter with Customs, but never pay it to the vendor if you have any doubts.

The question often crops up at the last minute on stock. This is usually paid for separately on the day of the takeover because the precise sum due can only be established by counting what is being handed over. Do not leave any possible argument about VAT until the day. Have your solicitor agree with the vendor's that no tax ought to be charged and get confirmation in writing.

Though this is a technical and somewhat obscure point, I stress the subject because getting it wrong has cost others a lot of money.

Your VAT registration

You will have to register immediately on taking over the shop. The registration limit is raised every year but is currently (1985) £19,500 annual turnover. It is an unusual shop which does not sell much more than that and, since there is already evidence for the sales in the vendor's records, you know that your own are likely to exceed the limit. Therefore you cannot wait until they have done so but must register at once.

Contact Customs before the day of the takeover and get the registration formalities out of the way. You will find their address under Customs and Excise in Yellow Pages. Customs will give you some leaflets about VAT, the records you have to keep etc. I urge you, however, to discuss what you need to do with your accountant before you take over the business, for the same reasons as, elsewhere, I have said you should discuss your records in general with him. After the takeover, you will have many other things to do and you will be very glad if you have already found out how to cope with the bookkeeping.

Another reason for dealing with your VAT registration in advance is to get your VAT number to print on any invoices you may need.

Choosing your retail scheme

A retail shop cannot calculate its output tax in the usual way because it does not issue tax invoices. It therefore has to use a 'retail scheme', which is a means of calculating how much VAT there is in the takings.

There are nine retail schemes but choosing one is not as complicated as that may make it sound. First, if you sell at only one rate of tax, you automatically use scheme A.

If you sell at two rates and therefore have to apportion your takings between them, there are a number of possible schemes for the smaller shop, of which the most common are F, B, D, and G.

Scheme F requires you to note your sales at each rate of tax as you put the money in the till. That is difficult to do in a busy shop and I advise you to avoid F, unless the nature of the business is such that you are sure that you can record the analysis of sales accurately.

Scheme B is often useful if you have only a minority of sales at zero rate or if, like a newsagent, many of your suppliers' invoices give you the retail values. You have to do some calculation work in valuing your zero-rated purchases at selling prices for scheme B.

Scheme D has a turnover limit, above which you cannot use it. This is occasionally increased by Customs so check what the current figure is at the time you buy the business. Scheme D is not accurate but it is a reasonable compromise between the need to keep extra records and the time this involves. The calculations are not difficult and do not take long.

Scheme G is very dangerous! This tends to be used by shops, whose sales are above the limit for scheme D. It normally results in them paying far too much output tax because of the way the calculations work. I do not have space to explain here exactly why this is so and, anyway, it is a technical subject. If you find the vendor is using scheme G, take advice before you go on doing so yourself.

It is up to you which retail scheme you use. The rules usually offer you a choice of several out of the nine. Each has various advantages and disadvantages. Unfortunately the Customs notice about the schemes does not explain what these are; Croner's *Reference Book for VAT* does in its retail schemes section. It goes into the pros and cons in detail. Your professional adviser may have access to a copy or you may find one in the reference section of your local library.

Since you know you will have to cope with VAT as a retailer, I suggest you get the main Customs notice about the retail schemes, together with the explanatory leaflets concerning schemes A, B, D, F and G and see what you make of them before you take over a business. As with so many other points, it will be easier to find the time to get advice from either Customs or your professional advisers before you have the business to run.

Your bank account

Your bank manager and your accountant will advise you whether you should open a separate business bank account. There are advantages in keeping the business transactions separate from your private ones, but it is often not necessary to have two accounts and it will cost you a little more.

Suppliers and customers

You may need to tell your principal suppliers and your customers of the changeover. If you are buying a retail shop, most of the customers will find out by coming into the shop. If it sells on credit, you must agree with the vendor how to arrange the formalities so that the customers know exactly what they owe him and on what date they start paying you. In the case of a small shop which has very few customers 'on tick', it may be appropriate for you to collect the cash and hand it over to the vendor. What you must not do is buy debts from him which you may not be able to collect. For one thing, he knows the customers and you do not.

It is wise not to allow goods on credit to retail customers. You will probably find that some of them come in saying that your predecessor allowed them to take stuff and to pay at the end of the week or month. Be very wary about this. It is an obvious ploy. The problem is that you are doing neither them nor yourself a service in allowing credit. It is the quickest way to *lose* a customer who is in financial trouble. The reason is that, having run up a bill with you which he cannot pay, he goes somewhere else and repeats the process. If you make him pay cash, you will at least ensure that he goes on buying from you when he is able to pay, instead of taking your goods for a short period and then never returning.

I mentioned suppliers earlier. Do not neglect the opportunity afforded by your taking over to ask what terms they can offer you. They will be anxious to please a new customer and you may be surprised at the help and minor concessions which they will make to you initially.

Are you taking over a limited company?

I explained what a company is in Chapter 4. If it is a company which you are buying, you are taking over not only its assets but also its liabilities. This means that you assume responsibility for the amounts owed to its creditors and for collecting the amounts due from its customers. If this is so, you must make sure that the accounts are accurate, otherwise you may find yourself having to pay out more than you expected and being unable to collect some of the debts due.

Physical security of the premises

The local police will advise you on this. Now is a good moment to do something about it before it becomes just another of those 'things you haven't quite got around to yet'. A break-in not only distracts your attention from more important things and causes you direct loss (depending on the amount reimbursed by your insurance company), but it can also lose you business as a result of not having stock available when it is wanted by customers. That can be much more serious in the long run.

Wages records

It is compulsory to give each employee a detailed pay slip which shows all deductions from gross pay. If you use a bound wages book you must write out a slip as a separate operation, though you can duplicate these, leaving only the figures to be entered. But there are 'one write' systems available from your local stationer which use carbon copies to produce the pay slips, individual pay record and weekly wages list in one operation. These save time if you have a number of employees.

Your basic accounting records

Before you take over check with your accountant what records he thinks you should keep. Do not leave this for a month or two until your papers are in chaos and you have failed to keep the right information. Start the job right. So many people make the mistake of waiting until they have traded for a year before taking their records to an accountant, by which time the mess costs much more to sort out. I write from experience, having spent a great deal of time trying to show small shopkeepers what records they should keep. The basics are as follows:

(a) A cash record showing the money you have received from customers and what you have done with it, ie the bills paid in cash. 'Cash' in this context means notes or coin, not 'paying cash' by writing out a cheque on delivery of goods, money paid into the bank and money still held.

(b) Your cheque book counterfoils completed to show what the cheques were written for.

(c) Any necessary VAT records.

(d) An invoice file, *not* a series of brown envelopes, on which are securely fastened all the bills which you pay. It helps to organise your records if you can file your expense invoices under 'goods for resale', 'rent', 'telephone', 'insurance' etc.

Good accounting records will save you both time and expense in accountant's fees. Apart from that and from your legal obligations to keep records, you may lose a great deal of money if you do not control your finances properly. This applies particularly to stocks and cash.

Be a 'new broom' but with discretion

Do not buy new equipment or make expensive alterations when you first move in, unless you are really sure of what you are doing. It is easy to waste money by choosing the wrong item or doing unnecessary work. Experience will quickly teach you what is needed and what is merely a frill.

Do, however, have a spring clean. Redecorating can be done relatively cheaply and it can transform the look of a place which has become a little dowdy.

Until they become used to the new owner, your customers will be a bit suspicious of you and it is normal for sales to fall off at first. But they will soon recover if you approach the job correctly. Meanwhile it is a good idea to attack the dirt and freshen up the premises before you get too used to them. Do not make any radical changes before you have been around long enough to know what will work best.

Questions on Chapter 10

1. Have you agreed with the vendor whether he is to reduce his stock of goods for resale by not reordering as usual?

2. Have you agreed beforehand on the method of valuing the stocks you take over?

3. If the method is to calculate values at retail and then use an average percentage to reduce them to cost, have you checked the percentages proposed with recent invoices from suppliers?

4. Do the percentages produce a cost figure *before* VAT? You should check that the percentages used to reduce from retail (which probably includes VAT) give the correct cost before VAT. Does the vendor agree that no VAT should be charged on either stock or other assets of the business, assuming that it is a going concern?

5. Are there are stocks which are unsaleable due to their age, condition, obsolescence etc? You should not expect to buy the vendor's mistakes — or at least not at full price.

6. Have you considered using an independent stocktaker to count and value the stocks on takeover?

7. Will you use the stock count as an opportunity not only

to examine the goods for condition etc, but also as a chance to find out where they are and what they are?

8. Are stock lists by supplier kept by the vendor to control his buying? Can you take these over or can you use the stocktaking to set up your own for this purpose?

9. Have you notified your motor insurers of the change of use for your vehicles?

10. Have you arranged insurance for any stock or cash which you may carry in your vehicle? An ordinary vehicle policy does not cover this.

11. Have you arranged to insure the assets of the business from the date of contract, *not* that of completion (ie takeover)?

12. Have you arranged your VAT registration if this is needed?

13. Have you decided whether you need to open a separate bank account for the business?

14. Have you arranged to contact all the main suppliers of goods to the business by visit, by meeting the sales representative, or by letter?

15. Does the business sell on credit? Do you need to write to customers telling them of the change and expressing your desire to continue doing business with them?

16. Will you write many business letters? Notepaper printed with your address and details of your trade looks businesslike and helps establish your standing.

17. Are you buying any debts due to the business (debtors)? If so, have you seen a complete list showing how long the amounts have been unpaid? Have you allowed for any likely bad debts?

18. Are you taking over the responsibility to pay any bills due by the business (creditors)? If so, have you verified the amounts with the creditors concerned as well as from the vendor's records?

19. If you sell on credit, have you arranged to have invoices printed? They are not essential but handwritten headings do not give a good impression. In a small business the

individual details may have to be written rather than typed. See also point 16.

20. There are legal requirements as to the information which invoices, letter headings etc must show according to the legal status of your business. A VAT number on your invoices is an example. Ask your professional advisers.

21. Have you considered the possibility of reducing the time needed to produce each invoice by printing repetitive details such as product names?

22. Will you also need monthly statements printed?

23. Will you need a licence under the Consumer Credit Act which applies to anyone advising or arranging credit for customers (such as hire purchase, leasing etc)? If you need a licence you should apply as soon as the contract is signed.

24. If selling your own house, have you arranged with your bank for bridging finance, if necessary, so that last-minute delays on that deal do not stop you completing your purchase?

25. Have you arranged for the immediate transfer of gas, electricity, telephone etc? An interruption in their supply because you have not completed the formalities could embarrass the business.

26. Is the physical security of the premises adequate? Should you improve the locks, bolts, fire equipment etc? Should you change the locks?

27. Have you considered the National Insurance position of your wife? She may be able to opt to pay reduced rate contributions provided you married before 5 April 1977. Reduced rate is not necessarily the right choice. Leaflet NI1 from the Social Security Office explains all this. Self-employed people must pay flat rate weekly contributions. You can arrange to have these charged to your bank account monthly by direct debit.

28. Have you reviewed your own life insurance policies?

29. Have you applied for the necessary trade licences?

30. Have you seen written evidence that the vendor has

cleared any outstanding hire purchase repayments on the equipment etc he is selling to you? Until he does, you cannot acquire a legal right to the goods.

31. If you will be employing staff, will you need to deduct from their wages under the PAYE system:
    (a) National Insurance contributions?
    (b) income tax?
    The weekly pay amount at which National Insurance becomes payable is lower than that applicable for tax. Both amounts alter as tax rates change. So check with your local Inspector of Taxes (in telephone directory under Inland Revenue).

32. If you do have to make deductions from wages, have you obtained the following stationery which you will need:
    (a) PAYE standard pack of cards etc from the Inland Revenue?
    (b) wages book and payslips from your local stationer?

33. Have you asked your accountant what accounting records you should keep?

Chapter 11

Sources of Information – Where You Can Get Help

Your professional advisers should be able to help you over many of the points in this book. But here are some sources of information and advice.

Libraries

Your librarian is there to help you and you will be astonished at the amount of information which he has on his shelves, or to which he has access from other libraries. Vast quantities of useful facts and figures are also obtainable from reference books.

Dotted around the country are a number of major business libraries and these obviously carry a much larger range of books than local centres (see the list below). Nevertheless, you may be surprised at what is on your doorstep.

The main business libraries
These specialise in business. Every county library also has a substantial business section.

Birmingham Central Library
Paradise
Birmingham B3 3HQ
021-235 4511

Business Library
The Mitchell Library
North Street
Glasgow G3 7DN
041-248 7121

The Central Library
William Brown Street
Liverpool L3 8EW
051-207 2147

The City Business Library
Gillett House
55 Basinghall Street
London EC2V 5BX
01-638 8215

Manchester Commercial Reference Library
Central Library
St Peter's Square
Manchester M2 5PD
061-228 0641

Sheffield Business Library
The Central Library
Surrey Street
Sheffield S1 1XZ
0742-734711

Small Firms Information Centres

The centres, set up by the Department of Trade and Industry, provide a free information service for small firms on any type of business problem. They also produce a number of useful pamphlets. Ask for freefone Enterprise (via the telephone operator) at no charge. The centres have telephone-answering machines so you can leave a query at any time and they will ring you back next day.

London and South Eastern Region
Ebury Bridge House
Ebury Bridge Road
London SW1W 8QD
01-730 8451

South Western Region
5th Floor
The Pithay
Bristol BS1 2NB
0272 294546

Northern Region
22 Newgate Shopping Centre
Newcastle upon Tyne NE1 1ZP
0632 325353

North Western Region
3rd Floor
320-325 Royal Exchange
Manchester M2 7AH
061-832 5282
and
1 Old Hall Street
Liverpool L3 9HJ
051-236 5756

Yorkshire and Humberside Region
1 Park Row
City Square
Leeds LS1 5NR
0532 445151

East Midlands Region
Severns House
Middle Pavement
Nottingham NG1 7DW
0602 506181

West Midlands Region
Ladywood House
Stephenson Street
Birmingham B2 4DT
021-643 3344

Eastern Region
24 Brooklands Avenue
Cambridge CB2 2BU
0223 63312

Northern Ireland
Northern Ireland Local Enterprise Development Unit
Lamont House
Purdys Lane
Newtownbreda
Belfast BT8 4AR
0232 691031

Scotland
Scottish Development Agency
(Small Businesses Division)
102 Telford Road
Edinburgh EH4 2NP
031-343 1911

Small Firms Service
57 Bothwell Street
Glasgow G2 6TU
041-248 6014

Wales
Welsh Development Agency
Treforest Industrial Estate
Pontypridd
Mid Glamorgan CF37 5UT
044 385 2666

Small Firms Service
16 St David's House
Wood Street
Cardiff CF1 1ER
0222 396116

The Council for Small Industries in Rural Areas

CoSIRA offers help and advice to businesses in English towns
and villages with a population under 10,000; it also runs courses
and offers financial help and advice. There is a local office in
every county.

Head Office:
Council for Small Industries in Rural Areas (CoSIRA)
141 Castle Street
Salisbury SP1 3TP
0722 336255

Business Ideas Letter

The Institute of Small Business
13 Golden Square
London W1R 4AL
01-437 4923

98

This is primarily a monthly newsletter about small business ideas in general, but it often has items about shops plus full-length articles on the basics of different trades. These can be a useful guide and information source. Subscribers can sometimes be helped with individual queries to which answers have not been found elsewhere. The 'Institute' is a privately owned commercial organisation.

The grocers' voluntary buying groups

Alliance Wholesale Group (Village brand), Mace, Maid Marion, Spar and VG are all names of voluntary buying groups. Independent shops trade under these names and buy most of their goods from the wholesaler sponsoring the scheme. The groups run special offers and their own advertising; various additional services are available from the wholesalers to the shops in the groups, such as advice on layout, finance etc. To locate the wholesaler who covers your area, in the name of a particular group, find a shop trading under the name and ask. Alternatively enquire at your Small Firms Information Centre.

The local representatives of the groups may be useful sources of information about shops which are for sale. Not all businesses are advertised and the representatives usually get to know at an early stage when a shop is about to become available.

Industry Training Boards

Many of these have closed, and the one most likely to be of help to retailers is:

The Hotel and Catering Industry Training Board
Ramsey House
Central Square
Wembley
Middlesex HA9 7AP
01-902 8865

Local business organisations

Some local chambers of trade publish useful journals or newsletters. On the whole, however, their services are primarily of use to those already in business. Some run extensive programmes of courses and other activities, though these tend not to interest small shopkeepers.

99

The College for the Distributive Trades
30 Leicester Square
London WC2H 7LE
01-839 1547
Runs full-time and part-time courses for independent retailers.
Suitable for beginners.

The National Union of Shopkeepers
Lynch House
91 Mansfield Road
Nottingham NG1 3FN
Provides various services to its members.

Trade associations

The association relevant to your trade probably offers various
services of interest, once you have a shop. Meanwhile its journal
may give you valuable background. See trade journals on page
104. Here is a list of the more likely associations.

Booksellers Association
154 Buckingham Palace Road
London SW1
01-730 8214

British Franchise Association
Franchise Chambers
75a Bell Street
Henley-on-Thames
Oxfordshire RG9 2BD
0491 578049

British Hardware Federation
20 Harborne Road
Edgbaston
Birmingham B15 3AB
021-454 4385

British Hotels Restaurants and Caterers Association
40 Duke Street
London W1M 6HR
01-499 6641

The British Independent Grocers Association
Federation House
17 Farnborough Street
Farnborough
Hants GU14 8AG
0252 515001

The Crafts Advisory Committee
8 Waterloo Place
London SW1Y 4AT
01-930 4811

Hairdressing Council
12 David House
45 High Street
London SE25 6HJ
01-771 6205

Incorporated Guild of Hairdressers
24 Woodbridge Road
Guildford
Surrey GU1 1DY
0483 67922

The Independent Footwear Retailers Association
109 Headstone Road
Harrow
Middlesex HA1 1PG
01-427 1545

National Association of Funeral Directors
57 Doughty Street
London WC1N 2NE
01-242 9388

National Association of Master Bakers, Confectioners and
    Caterers
21 Baldock Street
Ware
Herts SG12 9DH
0920 68061

National Dairyman's Association
19 Cornwall Terrace
London NW1 4QP
01-486 7244

National Federation of Fish Friers
Federation House
289 Dewsbury Road
Leeds LS11 5HW
0532 713291

National Federation of Hairdressers
11 Goldington Road
Bedford MK40 3JY
0234 60332

National Federation of Retail Newsagents
2 Bridewell Place
London EC4V 6AR
01-353 6816

National Market Traders Federation
Yorkshire Bank Chambers
Loundside
Chapeltown
Sheffield S30 4UP
0742 465395

National Pharmaceutical Association Ltd
Mallinson House
40-42 St Peter's Street
St Albans
Herts AL1 3NT
0727 32161

Radio, Electrical and TV Retailers Association (RETRA) Ltd
RETRA House
57-61 Newington Causeway
London SE1 6BE
01-403 1463

Retail Confectioners and Tobacconists Association
Ashley House
53 Christchurch Avenue
London N12 0DH
01-445 6344

Retail Fruit Trade Federation
108-10 Market Tower
Nine Elms Lane
London SW8 5NS
01-720 9168

Trade journals

There are literally hundreds of trade journals. Below are some of those most likely to interest a retailer. Certain publishers produce a number of different periodicals. To avoid repetition, the publishers' addresses are given below.

Benn Publications Ltd
Sovereign Way
Tonbridge
Kent TN9 1RW
0732 364422

IPC Consumer Industries Press Ltd
Quadrant House
The Quadrant
Sutton
Surrey SM2 5AS
01-661 3078

Retail Journals Ltd
Queensway House
2 Queensway
Redhill
Surrey RH1 1QS
0737 68611

The following are *trade* journals read primarily by business people. Some activities (especially hobbies like crafts and models) are covered by consumer magazines and are not listed for reasons of space; they can usually be found at your local newsagent. Most trade journals, on the other hand, are on subscription only.

Bakers' Review
(Official Journal of the National Association of Master Bakers,
  Confectioners and Caterers)
Penn House
Penn Place
Rickmansworth
Herts WD3 1SF
0923 777000

The Bookseller
12 Dyott Street
London WC1A 1DF
01-836 8911

Cabinet Maker and Retail Furnisher
Benn Publications Ltd

Carpet and Floor Coverings Review
Benn Publications Ltd

Caterer and Hotelkeeper
IPC Consumer Industries Press Ltd

Catering Times
IPC Consumer Industries Press Ltd

Catering and Hotel Management
Link House
9 Dingwall Avenue
Croydon CR9 2TA
01-686 2599

Chemist and Druggist
Benn Publications Ltd

Craft and Hobby Dealer
5 Station Road
Andoversford
Cheltenham
Glos GL54 4LA
0242 820400

Do It Yourself Retailing
The Link House Group
Dingwall Avenue
Croydon CR9 2TA
01-686 2599

Drapers' Record
Textile Trade Publications Ltd
Knightway House
20 Soho Square
London W1V 6DT
01-734 1255

Electrical and Electronic Trader
IPC Consumer Industries Press Ltd

Electrical and Radio Trading
IPC Consumer Industries Press Ltd

Fashion Weekly
6 Cambridge Gate
London NW1 4JR
01-486 0155

Fish Friers' Review
(National Federation of Fish Friers)
Federation House
289 Dewsbury Road
Leeds LS11 5HW
0532 712011

Fish Trader
(Official Journal of the National Federation of Fishmongers)
Retail Journals Ltd

Frozen and Chilled Foods
Retail Journals Ltd

Funeral Director
(National Association of Funeral Directors)
57 Doughty Street
London WC1N 2NE
01-242 9388

Fur Weekly News
122 Lea Bridge Road
London E5 9RB
01-248 5949

The Grocer
5-7 Southwark Street
London SE1 1RQ
01-407 6981

Hairdressers' Journal International
IPC Consumer Industries Press Ltd

Hardware Today
(The British Hardware Federation Journal)
20 Harborne Road
Edgbaston
Birmingham B15 3AB
021-454 4385

Hardware Trade Journal
Benn Publications Ltd

Independent Grocer
Blair House
184-186 High Street
Tonbridge
Kent TN9 1BE

Meat Trader Viewpoint
(Official Journal of the National Federation of Meat Traders)
1 Belgrove
Tunbridge Wells
Kent TN1 1YW
0892 41412

Meat Trades Journal
Northwood House
93-99 Goswell Road
London EC1V 7QA
01-253 9355

Men's Wear
Textile Trade Publications Ltd
Knightway House
20 Soho Square
London W1V 6DT
01-734 1255

The Milk Industry
(Journal of the National Dairyman's Association)
18-19 Cornwall Terrace
London NW1 4QP
01-486 7244

Motor Trader
IPC Consumer Industries Press Ltd

National Hairdresser
(Official Journal of the National Federation of Hairdressers)
38 Charlotte Street
London W1P 1HP
01-637 9794

Newsagent
38-42 Hampton Road
Teddington
Middx TW11 0JE
01-977 8787

Nurseryman and Garden Centre
Benn Publications Ltd

Off Licence News
5-7 Southwark Street
London SE1 1RQ
01-407 6981

Pet Store Trader
Clergy House
Churchyard
Ashford
Kent TN23 1QW
0233 36656

Pharmaceutical Journal
1 Lambeth High Street
London SE1 7JN
01-735 9141

Retail Confectioner and Tobacconist
(Journal of the Retail Confectioners and Tobacconists
    Association)
CTN Enterprises Ltd
53 Christchurch Avenue
London N12 0DH
01-445 6344

Retail Fruit Trade Review
(Retail Fruit Trade Federation)
108-10 Market Tower
1 Nine Elms Lane
London SW8 5NS
01-720 9168

Retail Jeweller
Knightway House
20 Soho Square
London W1V 6DT
01-439 9841

Retail Newsagent, Tobacconist and Confectioner
(Official Journal of the National Federation of Retail
    Newsagents)
News and Book Trade Review & Stationer's Gazette Limited
60-66 Saffron Hill
London EC1N 8QX
01-404 3136

Service Station
Service Station Publications Ltd
178-202 Great Portland Street
London W1N 6NH
01-637 2400

Sports Trader
Benn Publications Ltd

Stamp Magazine
The Link House Group
Dingwall Avenue
Croydon CR9 2TA
01-686 2599

Toy Trader
Penn House
Penn Place
Rickmansworth
Herts WD3 1SN
0923 777000

Travel Agency
Maclean Hunter Ltd
76 Oxford Street
London W1N 0HH
01-434 2233

Finding your shop

It may seem illogical to leave this until last. However, the main sources, your local paper and local estate agents, will be known to you or can easily be located through the Yellow Pages.

Regional papers, such as the *Yorkshire Post*, tend to carry advertisements for businesses over a wider area than the small town paper, but there is no national publicity for small shops in the true sense. The principal newspapers may carry occasional ads, but these are mainly for properties in the south of England.

Dalton's Weekly and the *London Weekly Advertiser*, both of which are available from your newsagent, carry extensive advertising but are also southern-based.

Business transfer agents can be found in the Yellow Pages. They are estate agents who specialise in selling businesses, with or without freehold property. Many ordinary estate agents know little about businesses. They only deal with them if there is freehold property attached and then as a sideline. Certain transfer agents specialise in particular types of shop business, such as sub post offices or hotels. If you study your local press, check in the Yellow Pages and ask around, you will soon find out who deals with what in your area. See also page 99, 'The grocers' voluntary buying groups'.

Index